Introduction

Study Skills – what you need to know to pass exams!

Pause for thought

Many students might skip quickly through a page like this. After all, we all know how to revise. Do you really though?

Think about this:

"IF YOU ALWAYS DO WHAT YOU ALWAYS DO, YOU WILL ALWAYS GET WHAT YOU HAVE ALWAYS GOT."

Do you like the grades you get? Do you want to do better? If you get full marks in your assessment, then that's great! Change nothing! This section is just to help you get that little bit better than you already are.

There are two main parts to the advice on offer here. The first part highlights fairly obvious things but which are also very important. The second part makes suggestions about revision that you might not have thought about but which WILL help you.

Part 1

DOH! It's so obvious but …

Start revising in good time

Don't leave it until the last minute – this will make you panic.

Make a revision timetable that sets out work time AND play time.

Sleep and eat!

Obvious really, and very helpful. Avoid arguments or stressful things too – even games that wind you up. You need to be fit, awake and focused!

Know your place!

Make sure you know exactly **WHEN and WHERE** your exams are.

Know your enemy!

Make sure you know what to expect in the exam.

How is the paper structured?

How much time is there for each question?

What types of question are involved?

Which topics seem to come up time and time again?

Which topics are your strongest and which are your weakest?

Are all topics compulsory or are there choices?

Learn by DOING!

There is no substitute for past papers and practice papers – they are simply essential! Tackling this collection of papers and answers is exactly the right thing to be doing as your exams approach.

Part 2

People learn in different ways. Some like low light, some bright. Some like early morning, some like evening / night. Some prefer warm, some prefer cold. But everyone uses their BRAIN and the brain works when it is active. Passive learning – sitting gazing at notes – is the most INEFFICIENT way to learn anything. Below you will find tips and ideas for making your revision more effective and maybe even more enjoyable. What follows gets your brain active, and active learning works!

Activity 1 – Stop and review

Step 1

When you have done no more than 5 minutes of revision reading STOP!

Step 2

Write a heading in your own words which sums up the topic you have been revising.

Step 3

Write a summary of what you have revised in no more than two sentences. Don't fool yourself by saying, "I know it, but I cannot put it into words". That just means you don't know it well enough. If you cannot write your summary, revise that section again, knowing that you must write a summary at the end of it. Many of you will have notebooks full of blue/black ink writing. Many of the pages will not be especially attractive or memorable so try to liven them up a bit with colour as you are reviewing and rewriting. **This is a great memory aid, and memory is the most important thing.**

Activity 2 — Use technology!

Why should everything be written down? Have you thought about "mental" maps, diagrams, cartoons and colour to help you learn? And rather than write down notes, why not record your revision material?

What about having a text message revision session with friends? Keep in touch with them to find out how and what they are revising and share ideas and questions.

Why not make a video diary where you tell the camera what you are doing, what you think you have learned and what you still have to do? No one has to see or hear it, but the process of having to organise your thoughts in a formal way to explain something is a very important learning practice.

Be sure to make use of electronic files. You could begin to summarise your class notes. Your typing might be slow, but it will get faster and the typed notes will be easier to read than the scribbles in your class notes. Try to add different fonts and colours to make your work stand out. You can easily Google relevant pictures, cartoons and diagrams which you can copy and paste to make your work more attractive and **MEMORABLE**.

Activity 3 – This is it. Do this and you will know lots!

Step 1

In this task you must be very honest with yourself! Find the SQA syllabus for your subject (www.sqa.org.uk). Look at how it is broken down into main topics called MANDATORY knowledge. That means stuff you MUST know.

Step 2

BEFORE you do ANY revision on this topic, write a list of everything that you already know about the subject. It might be quite a long list but you only need to write it once. It shows you all the information that is already in your long-term memory so you know what parts you do not need to revise!

Step 3

Pick a chapter or section from your book or revision notes. Choose a fairly large section or a whole chapter to get the most out of this activity.

With a buddy, use Skype, Facetime, Twitter or any other communication you have, to play the game "If this is the answer, what is the question?". For example, if you are revising Geography and the answer you provide is "meander", your buddy would have to make up a question like "What is the word that describes a feature of a river where it flows slowly and bends often from side to side?".

Make up 10 "answers" based on the content of the chapter or section you are using. Give this to your buddy to solve while you solve theirs.

Step 4

Construct a wordsearch of at least 10 X 10 squares. You can make it as big as you like but keep it realistic. Work together with a group of friends. Many apps allow you to make wordsearch puzzles online. The words and phrases can go in any direction and phrases can be split. Your puzzle must only contain facts linked to the topic you are revising. Your task is to find 10 bits of information to hide in your puzzle, but you must not repeat information that you used in Step 3. DO NOT show where the words are. Fill up empty squares with random letters. Remember to keep a note of where your answers are hidden but do not show your friends. When you have a complete puzzle, exchange it with a friend to solve each other's puzzle.

Step 5

Now make up 10 questions (not "answers" this time) based on the same chapter used in the previous two tasks. Again, you must find NEW information that you have not yet used. Now it's getting hard to find that new information! Again, give your questions to a friend to answer.

Step 6

As you have been doing the puzzles, your brain has been actively searching for new information. Now write a NEW LIST that contains only the new information you have discovered when doing the puzzles. Your new list is the one to look at repeatedly for short bursts over the next few days. Try to remember more and more of it without looking at it. After a few days, you should be able to add words from your second list to your first list as you increase the information in your long-term memory.

FINALLY! Be inspired...

Make a list of different revision ideas and beside each one write **THINGS I HAVE** tried, **THINGS I WILL** try and **THINGS I MIGHT** try. Don't be scared of trying something new.

And remember – "FAIL TO PREPARE AND PREPARE TO FAIL!"

Higher Physical Education

The advice below will help you make sense of what Higher Physical Education is all about in terms of course structure and grading. It will also offer you sound advice about the final exam.

The course

The Higher Physical Education course has been designed to provide progression from both the Credit level award in Standard Grade Physical Education and from the Intermediate 2 course. The Higher course provides the opportunity for personal challenge and fulfillment through improving performance while developing knowledge and understanding about performance. It is made up of two mandatory units:

- Performance
- Analysis and Development of Performance.

Performance

This unit assessment is a practical assessment carried out through observation or by video. Assessment is based on your performance in at least one activity and it should be conducted on an occasion near the end of the course. To achieve a unit pass you must score 11 marks or more in one activity.

Analysis and Development of Performance

This unit consists of structured questions in one activity and provides the opportunity to assess process knowledge and concept knowledge in one area of analysis. To pass this unit you must provide evidence of this process and concept knowledge. This is often achieved through completion of a NAB set by the SQA or your school.

How the course is graded

To gain a course award you must pass the units as well as the course assessment.

In the course assessment, you will develop your performance in a minimum of two activities taught within school. Each activity will be marked out of 20 marks giving each candidate a score out of 40 marks. The external exam is worth 60 marks. The two marks are combined for an overall score for the course grading

The exam

The Higher exam is 2 hours and 30 minutes long. It is made up of 8 questions – two questions are set from each of the following Areas of Analysis:

- Performance Appreciation
- Preparation of the Body
- Skills and Techniques
- Structures, Strategies and Composition

You must answer three questions each from a different Area of Analysis. In each Area there is a choice of two questions. Each question is worth 20 marks and is usually made up of four parts – (a), (b), (c) and (d). Each part is usually worth either four or six marks.

At Higher level, the exam is set in a structured manner where candidates are required to demonstrate both width and depth of key concept knowledge. Many candidates have difficulty in achieving this.

The most common mistake candidates make in the Higher paper is the lack of detail and depth of answer required to show both acquired knowledge (knowledge you have learned) and applied knowledge (using the knowledge you have learned).

On your course you will learn how to identify your strengths and weaknesses and be able to choose and apply appropriate methods of practice or training to hopefully improve your performance in individual, team, skill, fitness, strategy and tactics contexts.

All of the questions are built around the cycle of analysis. You may be asked questions on any part of the cycle. For example, you may be asked to describe how you collected data on your performance, explain what you understand about stages of learning or discuss the training programme you used to improve your performance.

Where candidates are performing poorly

There are a number of command words in each question. These are usually:

- Describe (how you do it).
- Explain (how and why you do it).
- Discuss/justify (how, why, and justify and argue reasons why you do it).

There is evidence of candidates' responses lacking depth when they are asked to 'discuss' or 'justify' their answer. Many candidates still tend to 'describe' and/or 'explain' rather than show critical thinking in their answers. An example of this is where candidates are asked to discuss the course of action they took to improve a skill/technique that needed improving:

"In order to improve my smash in badminton, I carried out a feeder practice where my partner would repeatedly feed me high clears for me to smash (description). This allowed me to focus on my weakness of not turning sideways on and being able to transfer my weight forward without pressure (explanation). "

In this example, the candidate has described what they did and why they did it, but has not justified why they did it. Here is the discussion which should be added into the same answer.

"By repeating this movement over and over again I got used to performing the correct technique until I was able to perform the smash correctly and consistently. Gradually the feeder made me move to play the smash to put me under more game-like pressure."

The candidate has now discussed and justified why they did a feeder practice. Remember, the key to discussion is not just to say why you do something, but to be able to justify or argue why this is the case.

The other area where candidates answer poorly is when questions ask about monitoring. Monitoring relates to an ongoing process where you observe and check the progress or quality of something over a period of time. Many candidates answer that they collect data after they have finished their development programme rather than during it. Whilst they still gain some marks for this, the number awarded is usually in the lower range.

Where candidates do well

Candidates tend to answer well in questions where the command word is "describe".

For example, where a question asks candidates to describe methods to collect data on a particular skill or technique, candidates are able to describe in detail various methods of collecting data such as games analysis sheets, movement analysis sheets, scatter grams, focused analysis sheets and how to carry out these methods.

Candidates also answer well when asked to demonstrate acquired knowledge from their course. For example, candidates may be asked to describe or explain the fitness requirements for effective performance in an activity. Candidates are able to explain the physical, skill-related and mental fitness necessary for the activity chosen, demonstrating specific knowledge required to access the full range of marks. The section below will take you through some of the key areas and explain how you can best make use of the papers in this book.

Good exam technique

Before you start answering a question:

- Read the whole question paper.
- Read all parts of each question.
- Select the three Areas you know most about.
- From each area, select the question you think you can answer well.
- Plan the order you intend to answer them in.
- Share out your time effectively for each question.

- Highlight the command words, for example "describe" or "explain" …
- Try to have time left to check over your answers. This could save you some marks.

Do not attempt to apply pre-planned answers to examination questions. This approach restricts the depth of response given and often candidates then do not answer the question being addressed, resulting in them achieving very low marks. This has the effect of disadvantaging all candidates, preventing them from achieving the best possible mark for the whole question.

Good luck!

Remember that the rewards for passing Higher Physical Education are well worth it! Your pass will help you get the future you want for yourself. In the exam, be confident in your own ability. If you're not sure how to answer a question, trust your instincts and just give it a go anyway. Keep calm and don't panic! GOOD LUCK!

Official

SQA Past Papers

WITH ANSWERS

Higher
Physical Education

2010–2014

Hodder Gibson Study Skills Advice – General — page 3
Hodder Gibson Study Skills Advice –
Higher Physical Educaton — page 5
2010 EXAM — page 7
2011 EXAM — page 15
2012 EXAM — page 23
2013 EXAM — page 31
2014 EXAM — page 39
ANSWER SECTION — page 47

HODDER GIBSON
AN HACHETTE UK COMPANY

Hodder Gibson is grateful to the copyright holders, as credited on the final page of the Question Section, for permission to use their material. Every effort has been made to trace the copyright holders and to obtain their permission for the use of copyright material. Hodder Gibson will be happy to receive information allowing us to rectify any error or omission in future editions.

Hachette UK's policy is to use papers that are natural, renewable and recyclable products and made from wood grown in sustainable forests. The logging and manufacturing processes are expected to conform to the environmental regulations of the country of origin.

Orders: please contact Bookpoint Ltd, 130 Park Drive, Abingdon, Oxon OX14 4SE. Telephone: (44) 01235 827720. Fax: (44) 01235 400454.

Lines are open 9.00–5.00, Monday to Saturday, with a 24-hour message answering service. Visit our website at www.hoddereducation.co.uk. Hodder Gibson can be contacted direct on: Tel: 0141 848 1609; Fax: 0141 889 6315; email: hoddergibson@hodder.co.uk

This collection first published in 2014 by

Hodder Gibson, an imprint of Hodder Education,

An Hachette UK Company

2a Christie Street

Paisley PA1 1NB

{BrightRED Hodder Gibson is grateful to Bright Red Publishing Ltd for collaborative work in preparation of this book and all
PUBLISHING SQA Past Paper, National 5 and Higher for CfE Model Paper titles 2014.

Typeset by PDQ Digital Media Solutions Ltd, Bungay, Suffolk NR35 1BY

Printed in the UK

A catalogue record for this title is available from the British Library

ISBN 978-1-4718-3687-9

3 2 1

2015 2014

HIGHER

2010

[BLANK PAGE]

X205/301

NATIONAL	TUESDAY, 1 JUNE	PHYSICAL
QUALIFICATIONS	9.00 AM – 11.30 AM	EDUCATION
2010		HIGHER

Candidates should attempt **three** questions, each chosen from a different area.

AREA 1: PERFORMANCE APPRECIATION

Marks

Question 1

Choose an activity.

(a) Quality performance depends on:

- fluency
- economy of effort
- precision
- accuracy
- control.

Select **two** of the above and explain the importance of each.   **6**

(b) Why is it important to use an **integrated (combination) training approach** to develop whole performance? Justify your answer by giving examples from your programme.   **4**

(c) Discuss the importance of using short and long term goals. Give examples to support your answer.   **6**

(d) Describe the methods used to evaluate the success of the programme in achieving your goals.   **4**

(20)

Question 2

(a) Discuss the importance of considering models of performance when establishing training priorities.   **4**

Choose an activity.

(b) Describe the **nature** and **demands** of this activity.   **6**

(c) Describe your initial level of performance with reference to technical, physical, personal and special qualities.   **4**

(d) Select one of the qualities from part (c).

Discuss how a programme of work helped you to improve your overall level of performance. Give examples to support your answer.   **6**

(20)

AREA 2: PREPARATION OF THE BODY   *Marks*

Question 3

(*a*) Discuss why it is appropriate to train using each of the following approaches.

- Within the activity (conditioning)
- Outwith the activity
- Through a combination of both   **6**

Choose an activity.

(*b*) Explain how you planned and implemented your training programme.   **6**

(*c*) Describe **one** training session that you undertook to develop your personal level of performance.   **4**

(*d*) How did you monitor your progress within the training programme?   **4**

    (20)

Question 4

Choose an activity.

(*a*) Explain the importance of each of the following types of fitness in your chosen activity.

- Physical
- Skill-related
- Mental   **6**

(*b*) Select **one** aspect of fitness.

Describe **one** method you used to gather information on this aspect.   **4**

(*c*) Explain why the method used was both **valid** and **reliable.**   **4**

(*d*) Describe, briefly, one method of training to improve your performance in this activity. Discuss why this method was appropriate.   **6**

    (20)

[Turn over

AREA 3: SKILLS AND TECHNIQUES

Marks

Question 5

(a) Explain what you understand about the following.

- Information Processing model
- Skill classification

6

Choose an activity.

(b) Compare your whole performance to that of a model performance.

4

Select a skill or technique.

(c) Describe, in detail, the different methods of practice you used to develop this skill or technique.

6

(d) Discuss why it is important to monitor and review your development programme.

4

(20)

Question 6

(a) Explain what you understand about the stages of learning.

6

Choose an activity and a skill or technique.

(b) For one stage of learning, select a method of practice you used to develop this skill or technique. Explain why this method was appropriate.

4

(c) Select **two** of the following.

- Motivation
- Concentration
- Feedback

Discuss the importance of **both** when carrying out your development programme.

6

(d) Having developed this skill or technique, describe the effect this had on your whole performance.

4

(20)

AREA 4: STRUCTURES, STRATEGIES AND COMPOSITION

Marks

Question 7

Choose an activity.

(a) Describe a structure, strategy or composition you have used.   **4**

(b) What factors did you take into consideration when selecting this structure, strategy or composition?   **4**

(c) Describe briefly a situation where this structure, strategy or composition was not effective. Explain why this was the case in this situation.   **6**

(d) What changes/adaptations did you make to address this situation? Justify the actions that were taken.   **6**

(20)

Question 8

Choose an activity and structure, strategy or composition.

(a) (i) Describe **one** strength when performing in this structure, strategy or composition. Explain the effects this had on your performance.   **3**

    (ii) Describe **one** weakness when performing in this structure, strategy or composition. Explain the effects this had on your performance.   **3**

(b) Explain what you did to address the weakness identified in part (a) (ii).   **4**

(c) Describe how you evaluated the effectiveness of your performance in relation to the weakness identified in part (a) (ii).   **4**

(d) The following are key fundamentals when applying a structure, strategy or composition.

- Using space effectively in performance
- Using repetition, variation and contrast in performance
- Using creativity
- Width, depth and mobility

Select **two** of the above and explain the importance of each when applying your chosen structure, strategy or composition.   **6**

(20)

[END OF QUESTION PAPER]

[BLANK PAGE]

[BLANK PAGE]

X205/301

NATIONAL QUALIFICATIONS 2011	MONDAY, 30 MAY 9.00 AM – 11.30 AM	PHYSICAL EDUCATION HIGHER

Candidates should attempt **three** questions, each chosen from a different area.

Marks

AREA 1: PERFORMANCE APPRECIATION

Question 1

Choose an activity.

(a) Discuss how your **overall** performance compares to that of a model performance.   **6**

(b) Select **one** of the following performance qualities.

- Technical
- Physical
- Personal
- Special

Describe a programme of work you followed to improve this quality.   **4**

(c) How did you make the most of your strengths within this quality when performing?   **4**

(d) Why is it important to evaluate your overall performance following the programme of work described in part (b)? Describe how this evaluation was carried out.   **6**

(20)

Question 2

Choose an activity.

(a) Describe the **nature** of a quality performance in this activity.   **4**

(b) How did you prepare mentally for this quality performance?   **4**

(c) Describe, in detail, an **integrated** (combination) improvement programme that developed your performance.   **6**

(d) Discuss the improvements in your overall performance following this improvement programme.   **6**

(20)

Marks

AREA 2: PREPARATION OF THE BODY

Question 3

Choose an activity.

(a) Why is it important to gather information about your fitness **before** carrying out a training programme?   4

(b) Explain what you understand about the three phases of training.   6

(c) Select **one** phase of training. Describe a training programme you used to develop or maintain your fitness during this phase.   4

(d) Throughout the different phases of your training you will have set personal goals. Give examples of the goals you set.

Discuss the factors you considered when setting these goals.   6

(20)

Question 4

(a) Explain the importance of mental aspects of fitness to performance.   4

Choose an activity.

(b) Describe, in detail, the physical and skill-related aspects of fitness required for this activity.   6

(c) Discuss the principles of training you considered when planning a fitness programme.   6

(d) During your training programme you will have made changes. Explain why these changes were necessary.   4

(20)

[Turn over

Marks

AREA 3: SKILLS AND TECHNIQUES

Question 5

Choose an activity.

(a) Describe the information you gathered about your performance using **one** of the following approaches.

- Mechanical Analysis
- Movement Analysis
- Consideration of quality   4

(b) Explain why you considered this approach to be appropriate.   4

(c) Justify the course of action you took to improve your performance.   6

(d) Explain the importance of using different types of feedback when developing performance.   6

(20)

Question 6

(a) Explain the advantages of considering a model performance when developing performance.   4

Choose an activity and a skill or technique.

(b) Describe the strengths and/or weaknesses you found when applying this skill or technique.   4

(c) Discuss the **principles of effective practice** you considered when planning your development programme.   6

(d) Describe **one** method of practice you used to improve your performance.

Explain why this method was relevant.   6

(20)

Marks

AREA 4: STRUCTURES, STRATEGIES AND COMPOSITION

Question 7

Choose an activity and a structure, strategy or composition.

(a) Describe how you gathered information about your performance when applying this structure, strategy or composition.   **4**

(b) Explain why this structure, strategy or composition makes the best use of your performance strengths.   **6**

(c) Describe the problems you encountered when applying this structure, strategy or composition.   **4**

(d) Justify the decisions you took to develop your performance within this structure, strategy or composition.   **6**

      (20)

Question 8

Choose an activity.

(a) Describe **two different** structures, strategies or compositions you have used in this activity.   **6**

(b) Select **one** of these structures, strategies or compositions.
Explain the advantage(s) of using it in a performance situation.   **4**

(c) Explain the advantage(s) of using the **other** structure, strategy or composition in a performance situation.   **4**

(d) Discuss **one limitation of each** of these structures, strategies or compositions.   **6**

      (20)

[END OF QUESTION PAPER]

[BLANK PAGE]

HIGHER

2012

[BLANK PAGE]

X205/12/02

NATIONAL QUALIFICATIONS 2012	TUESDAY, 29 MAY 9.00 AM – 11.30 AM	PHYSICAL EDUCATION HIGHER

Candidates should attempt **three** questions, each chosen from a different area.

Marks

AREA 1: PERFORMANCE APPRECIATION

Question 1

(a) Why is it important to consider models of performance when identifying the **demands** of an activity?   **4**

Choose an activity.

(b) Describe the **physical** and **technical** demands of this activity.   **6**

(c) Discuss the mental factors you consider before and during performance.   **4**

(d) Explain how you planned and managed a performance improvement programme to develop the mental factors described in part (c).   **6**

(20)

Question 2

Choose an activity.

(a) Describe the **personal** and **special** qualities that are important to performance in your chosen activity.   **6**

(b) You will have used a performance improvement programme to develop the personal or special qualities described in part (a).

Justify why this programme was appropriate.   **4**

(c) Describe **one** method you used to evaluate the success of this programme.   **4**

(d) Discuss the importance of setting short and long-term goals to develop your whole performance. Give examples to support your answer.   **6**

(20)

Marks

AREA 2: PREPARATION OF THE BODY

Question 3

Choose an activity.

(a) Discuss the fitness requirements needed for effective performance in your chosen activity.   **6**

(b) Describe the improvements that took place in your whole performance as a result of your fitness training programme.   **4**

(c) Describe in detail the method(s) of training that helped you to achieve these improvements in your performance.   **6**

(d) Explain why the training method(s) was appropriate.   **4**

(20)

Question 4

Choose an activity.

(a) Discuss the importance of **one** type of fitness to your performance.   **4**

(b) Describe, in detail, a training programme that helped you develop the type of fitness discussed in part (a).   **6**

(c) Explain the importance of the other two types of fitness to your performance.   **4**

(d) Explain the importance of fitness assessment

• before starting a training programme;
• on completion of a training programme.   **6**

(20)

[Turn over

Marks

AREA 3: SKILLS AND TECHNIQUES

Question 5

(*a*) Explain what you understand about

  • closed skills;
  • open skills.   **6**

Choose an activity and a skill or technique.

(*b*) Give specific details of how your performance of this skill or technique compares to a model performance.   **4**

(*c*) Explain why motivation **and** concentration affect the development of this skill or technique.   **6**

(*d*) Discuss why it is important to monitor your progress while developing your performance.   **4**

                                                                                                           (20)

Question 6

(*a*) There are three stages of learning.

  For **each** stage, identify **one** method of practice used to develop performance. Justify why these methods are appropriate to each stage.   **6**

Choose an activity and a skill or technique.

(*b*) Describe the method(s) you used to gather information on your chosen skill or technique.   **4**

(*c*) Describe the development needs identified from the information gathered in part (*b*).   **4**

(*d*) Explain how you made use of the **principles of effective practice** within your programme of work.   **6**

                                                                                                           (20)

Marks

AREA 4: STRUCTURES, STRATEGIES AND COMPOSITION

Question 7

Choose an activity.

(a) Describe a structure, strategy or composition you have used in this activity. **4**

(b) Describe a situation where you had to adapt or change this structure, strategy or composition. **4**

(c) Explain the course of action you took to change/adapt this structure, strategy or composition. Describe the impact of these changes/adaptations on your whole performance. **6**

(d) Describe a method you used to evaluate the success of this course of action. Why was this method appropriate? **6**

(20)

Question 8

(a) Discuss the factors to consider when selecting structures, strategies or compositions. **6**

Choose an activity and a structure, strategy or composition.

(b) Describe your role within this structure, strategy or composition. **4**

(c) (i) Within your role, identify **one** strength when performing in this structure, strategy or composition. Explain the effect this had on your performance. **3**

    (ii) Within your role, identify **one** weakness when performing in this structure, strategy or composition. Explain the effect this had on your performance. **3**

(d) Describe the programme of work you followed to improve the weakness identified in part (c) (ii). **4**

(20)

[END OF QUESTION PAPER]

[BLANK PAGE]

[BLANK PAGE]

X205/12/02

NATIONAL QUALIFICATIONS 2013	TUESDAY, 4 JUNE 9.00 AM – 11.30 AM	PHYSICAL EDUCATION HIGHER

Candidates should attempt **three** questions, each chosen from a different area.

Marks

AREA 1: PERFORMANCE APPRECIATION

Question 1

Choose an activity.

(a) Describe in detail the **nature** and **demands** of a quality performance in this activity.

6

(b) Describe your **whole** performance in comparison to a model performance in this activity.

4

(c) Briefly outline a training programme you have undertaken to improve your performance.

Discuss why it was necessary to consider both your **strengths** and **development needs** when devising this training programme.

6

(d) The mental factors which influence performance are:

- aggression (controlled)
- anxiety (state of arousal)
- concentration
- confidence.

Select **two** of these factors and explain their importance when performing.

4

(20)

Question 2

Choose an activity.

(a)
- Imagination
- Flair
- Disguise/deception
- Creativity

Select **one** of the above **special** performance qualities and explain the importance of this when performing within your chosen activity.

4

(b) Explain why **physical, personal and technical** qualities are required for effective performance in your chosen activity.

6

(c) Describe in detail an **integrated** (combination) improvement programme that developed your performance.

6

(d) Discuss the reasons why you would collect information on your performance before starting a programme of work.

4

(20)

Marks

AREA 2: PREPARATION OF THE BODY

Question 3

(*a*) Explain why **each** of the following principles of training are important when planning and implementing a training programme:

- specificity
- progressive overload.   6

Choose an activity.

(*b*) Select a physical related aspect of fitness which was a weakness. Explain the effect this had on your performance.   4

(*c*) Select a skill related aspect of fitness which was a weakness. Explain the effect this had on your performance.   4

(*d*) Describe in detail **one** training session you used to develop the physical **or** skill related aspect of fitness described in part (*b*) **or** (*c*).   6

(20)

Question 4

Choose an activity.

(*a*) There are **three** types of fitness:

- physical
- skill related
- mental.

Select **one** aspect of fitness from **each** of the types of fitness. Explain why each aspect is important for effective performance in your chosen activity.   6

(*b*) Select **one** of the aspects of fitness from part (*a*). Describe in detail a programme of work you used to develop this aspect.   6

(*c*) During your training you will have had to make changes to your programme of work. Discuss why these changes were necessary.   4

(*d*) Explain why it is important to monitor your progress when carrying out your programme of work.   4

(20)

[Turn over

Marks

AREA 3: SKILLS AND TECHNIQUES

Question 5

Choose an activity.

(a) Describe one method you used to collect information on your **whole** performance. Explain why this method was appropriate.   **4**

Choose a skill or technique.

(b) Describe a **different** method you used to collect information on this **skill or technique**. Explain why this different method was appropriate.   **4**

(c) Discuss why you applied the **principles of effective practice** as you worked to develop your performance.   **6**

(d) Explain the importance of feedback, concentration and motivation when developing performance.   **6**

(20)

Question 6

Choose an activity.

(a) Describe the strengths you identified in your **whole performance**.   **4**

Choose a skill or technique.

(b) Describe the specific weakness(es) you identified within this skill or technique. Explain the effects of these weakness(es) on your performance.   **6**

(c) Justify the methods of practice you used to improve your weakness(es) in this skill or technique.   **6**

(d) Explain what you understand about:

- simple skills
- complex skills.   **4**

(20)

Marks

AREA 4: STRUCTURES, STRATEGIES AND COMPOSITION

Question 7

Choose an activity.

(a) Describe **two** structures, strategies or compositions that you have used in this activity.   **6**

Select **one** of the structures, strategies or compositions described in part (a).

(b) Describe the problem(s) you encountered when applying this structure, strategy or composition.   **4**

(c) Justify the programme of work you carried out to overcome the problem(s).   **4**

(d) With particular reference to the programme of work you carried out, explain the impact this had on your whole performance. Describe briefly what you now consider to be your future development needs.   **6**

(20)

Question 8

(a) Explain the importance of **two** of the features listed below when applying a structure, strategy or composition:

- being perceptive
- making good decisions when under pressure
- being creative
- width/depth/mobility
- using space
- tempo/speed.   **6**

Choose an activity and a structure, strategy or composition.

(b) Describe your role within this structure, strategy or composition.   **4**

(c) Explain why this role makes best use of your performance strengths.   **4**

(d) Briefly describe an alternative structure, strategy or composition that you have used. Justify why you chose to use this other structure, strategy or composition.   **6**

(20)

[END OF QUESTION PAPER]

[BLANK PAGE]

HIGHER

2014

[BLANK PAGE]

X205/12/02

NATIONAL
QUALIFICATIONS
2014

MONDAY, 2 JUNE
9.00 AM – 11.30 AM

PHYSICAL
EDUCATION
HIGHER

Candidates should attempt **three** questions, each chosen from a different area.

Marks

AREA 1: PERFORMANCE APPRECIATION

Question 1

(a) Describe the personal and special demands of a quality performance in an activity of your choice.　**4**

(b) Describe **either** the technical or physical demands of a quality performance in an activity of your choice.　**4**

Choose an activity.

(c) Discuss how your **overall** performance compares to that of a model performance.　**6**

(d) What course of action would you take to improve your performance? Explain your reasons for this course of action.　**6**

(20)

Question 2

(a) Explain the importance of managing emotions before, during and after performance.　**6**

Choose an activity.

(b) Select **two** of the following performance qualities:

- Timing
- Speed
- Determination
- Flair

Explain the importance of each quality when performing.　**4**

(c) Select **one** of the qualities highlighted in Part (b). Describe how you gathered information about this quality during your overall performance.　**4**

(d) Discuss what you should take into account when setting short, medium and long term goals to develop performance.　**6**

(20)

Marks

AREA 2: PREPARATION OF THE BODY

Question 3

Choose an activity.

(a) Explain the importance of **two** aspects of mental fitness to your performance.   **4**

(b) Explain the importance of **two** aspects of skill-related fitness to your performance.   **4**

(c) Discuss the principles of training you considered when planning a fitness programme.   **6**

(d) Describe **one** method of training to improve your performance in this activity. Discuss why this method was appropriate.   **6**

(20)

Question 4

(a) There are **three** phases of training:

- **preparation** (pre season)
- **competition** (during the season)
- **transition** (off season).

Discuss why your training might differ between each of the phases. Give examples to support your answer.   **6**

Choose an activity.

(b) Select an aspect of fitness. Describe how you assessed this aspect of fitness both **within** and **outwith** your chosen activity.   **6**

(c) Describe **one** training session that you undertook to develop your personal level of performance.   **4**

(d) Why is it important to monitor and review your programme of work?   **4**

(20)

[Turn over

Marks

AREA 3: SKILLS AND TECHNIQUES

Question 5

(a) When learning and developing a skill, it is important to work through the three stages of learning. These are:

- the **preparation/cognitive stage**
- the **practice/associative stage**
- the **automatic/autonomous stage**.

Explain what you understand about **each** stage.   6

Choose an activity and a skill or technique.

(b) For **one** stage of learning, select a method of practice you used to develop this skill or technique. Explain why this method was appropriate.   4

(c) Describe the strengths and/or weaknesses you found when applying this skill or technique.   4

(d) Justify the course of action you took to improve your performance.   6

          (20)

Question 6

Choose an activity and a skill or technique.

(a) Explain the advantages of considering a model performance when developing performance.   4

(b) Describe **one** method of practice you used to improve your performance. Explain why this method was relevant.   6

(c) Having developed this skill/technique, discuss the **effect** that this has had on your **whole** performance.   4

(d) Select **two** of the following.

- Motivation
- Concentration
- Feedback

Discuss the importance of **both** when carrying out your development programme.   6

          (20)

Marks

AREA 4: STRUCTURES, STRATEGIES AND COMPOSITION

Question 7

Choose an activity.

(*a*) Describe a structure, strategy or composition that you have used.   **4**

(*b*) Discuss why this structure, strategy or composition makes the best use of your performance strengths.   **6**

(*c*) Describe your weakness(es) when applying this structure, strategy or composition. Discuss the effect that this had on your performance.   **6**

(*d*) Explain what you did to reduce the effect of the weakness(es) identified in part (*c*).   **4**

(20)

Question 8

Select **two** Structures, Strategies or Compositions from the same activity.

(*a*) Describe the benefits of **one** of these structures, strategies or compositions.   **4**

(*b*) Explain the limitations of the **other** structure, strategy or composition.   **4**

(*c*) Discuss why it is important to gather information about your performance when applying this structure, strategy or composition. Give examples of the strengths and weaknesses you identified.   **6**

(*d*) Justify the decisions you took to develop your performance within this structure, strategy or composition.   **6**

(20)

[END OF QUESTION PAPER]

[BLANK PAGE]

HIGHER | ANSWER SECTION

SQA HIGHER PHYSICAL EDUCATION 2010–2014

HIGHER PHYSICAL EDUCATION 2010

In the Higher Physical Education examination candidates will answer from the perspective of their experiences in a wide variety of activities. An activity specific answer section would result in an enormous document which would be extremely cumbersome and time-consuming to use and which could never realistically cover all possibilities.

In relation to **all** questions it should be noted that the relevance of the content in the candidates' responses will depend on:

- the activity selected
- the performance focus
- the training/development programme/programme of work selected
- the practical experiences of their course as the contexts for answers.

PERFORMANCE APPRECIATION

1. (a) *A good response should include some or most of the points as outlined below. The candidate's response should demonstrate detailed knowledge of the importance of each.*

   Special Performance Qualities: The responses will be wide ranging and relevant to the activity selected. Candidates may demonstrate acquired Knowledge and Understanding in respect of the specific role/solo related demands necessary for an effective performance.

   Reference to the application of a series of complex skills will impact on performance in competitive situations. For example, in relation to **role demands**,...*as a central defender I am pushed to my limits in the later stages of the game...it is essential that I time my tackles or I will give away penalties...I need to control the ball artistically to wrong foot my opponent and get the ball out of danger areas...etc.*

   In relation to **solo demands**...*as a gymnast I know that my tumbling routine has many complex skills that need to be performed in a linked sequence...I need tremendous focus as often I will be pushing myself to the limits...etc...most importantly I need to add flair and fluency in my routine to attract the best marks from the judges...etc.*

   For example, *in tennis my high level of **accuracy** when placing my second serve enabled me to maintain serving advantage even though my first serve had failed. I was confident that I could place the ball accurately and with the correct amount of spin. This makes it very difficult for my opponent to play a winning return. This had the added advantage of allowing me to be ambitious with my first serve and resulted in me hitting aces. This accuracy was achieved by...Accuracy was also very important when... ... ...*

   (b) *A good response should include some or most of the points as outlined below. The candidate should demonstrate acquired KU and support this with relevant examples.*

   The training programme offered may reflect the development of a technical and skill related quality/demand being developed (or any other relevant combinations). For example, in badminton: the aim = to develop the drop shot WHILST developing improved footwork (agility). The response should include relevant facts; train in the activity using repetition drills – moving to take feeds from right &

left hand side of court - combine with footwork drill, eg from T to various numbered areas of court... Progress to combination/conditioned rallies to ensure refinement of shot ie efficiency, accuracy and disguised placement as a result of energy efficient movement to meet the shot with balance and poise to execute the shot and return to base ready for the next shot etc.

A good response will typically include other relevant factors to demonstrate Knowledge and Understanding such as, progression, model performers, feedback, target setting, work to rest considerations, stages of learning, complexity of technique being developed, factors affecting performance, principles of training and or effective practice.

(c) *A good response should include some or most of the points as outlined below. The candidate's response should include detailed discussion to demonstrate thorough KU.*

Setting goals: A good response will highlight the importance of establishing short term goals to help reach longer term goals. Detailed examples should be offered to show understanding about performance gains as a result of setting realistic/attainable goals. For example, ...*inspires/ motivates to do better...lets you see if training is working/needs to be progresses...enables comparisons to be made...is a form of feedback...establishes achievement...can be used to judge performance against success criteria...etc.*

(d) *A good response should include some or most of the points as outlined below. Detailed description of **more than one** method is required. A maximum mark of 2 will be awarded for a detailed answer on only one method.*

The importance of monitoring and reviewing: A good response will highlight the differences/benefits of the purpose of monitoring = ongoing process. The candidate may provide qualitative or quantitative details of whether the programme is effective/working, it substantiates specific fitness/skill progress, it makes sure that overload/progressions can be applied as appropriate, etc. Reference to appropriate data methods to facilitate comparison of improvements, enables changes/adaptations to be made during my programme, achieving targets set, gaining and acting on feedback, aids motivation, ensures further challenge and progress. Importantly, the response must include reference to reviewing performance = summative process. Many candidates will repeat or include some of the previously mentioned comments. However reference to the evaluation of the whole process ie the impact of the training/development programme/programme of work should be highlighted. Judgements on the success/effectiveness of the programme/ used PLUS judgements on the success/effectiveness to whole performance must be clearly defined.

2. (a) *A good response should include some or most of the points as outlined below. In discussion the focus should be on how relevant KU was applied "when establishing training priorities"*

Model performance comparison: A good response will include reference to the range and qualities that are evident in a model performer's repertoire. Reference may be made across the range of demands required in performance ie technical, physical, skill and mental related.
In relation the demand selected relevant points may come from both 'like/unlike' perspective. For example, *unlike a Model Performer I do not have a repertoire of skills to meet the technical demands of... I fail to execute my...at the correct time*

and lack consistency, fluency. Unlike the Model Performer I look clumsy by comparison and lack economy of movement…they make everyone look so effortless…their movements/application of skills are used at the right time. However like the Model Performer I can manage my emotions/rarely display bad temper and concentrate fully on my game/role…etc.

The use of Model performance:

A good response will include reference to the impact on learning and or developing a specific part of their performance. Most likely this will pertain to skill learning/development. For example, using a model performer can advantage performance or developmental process in a number of ways.

- Identifies strengths and weaknesses.
- Increases confidence, motivation.
- Provides various types of feedback; qualitative, quantitive, diagnostic etc.
- Provides challenge in practice/competition.
- Provides accurate feeds continuously.
- Inspire to achieve higher levels of achievement.
- Supports planning practices/targets.
- Inspires to copy ideas.

For example, *I watched model performers in my class…I was inspired by them and wanted to be as good as they were…When perfecting my right hand lay-up I got feedback from them and they provided me with 1v1 challenge…this level of direct competition helped as a form of target setting; this kept me motivated and determined to do better…I gained in confidence and felt that my technique had greatly improved as a result…I… etc I used.*

(b) *A good response should include some or most of the points as outlined below. The **specific** nature of the activity and an **expansive range** of demands should be described.*

Nature: Individual/team. The duration of the game/event. The number of player(s)/performers involved. A spectator/audience event. Indoor/outdoor. Directly/indirectly competitive. Objective/subjective scoring systems in application. Codes of conduct.

Demands: Technical, Physical, Mental and Special. Candidates may demonstrate acquired Knowledge and Understanding across all related demands or focus on one more comprehensively. Similarly, candidates may demonstrate acquired Knowledge and Understanding in respect of the unique game/event demands or emphasise the demands unique to the role/solo/duo performance relative to the activity selected.

Special Performance Qualities: The responses will be wide ranging and relevant to the activity selected. Candidates may demonstrate acquired Knowledge and Understanding in respect of the specific role/solo related demands necessary for an effective performance.

Reference to the application of a series of complex skills will impact on performance in competitive situations. For example, *in relation to role demands,…as a central defender I am pushed to my limits in the later stages of the game…it is essential that I time my tackles or I will give away penalties…I need to control the ball artistically to wrong foot my opponent and get the ball out of danger areas…etc.* In relation to solo demands…*as a gymnast I know that my tumbling routine has many complex skills that need to be performed in a linked sequence…I need tremendous focus as often I will be pushing myself to the limits…etc…most importantly I need to add flair and fluency in my routine to attract the best marks from the judges…etc.*

Candidates, who are elite performers may demonstrate acquired Knowledge and Understanding in respect of the application of strategy/composition at appropriate times to ensure effective performance. Often this link is made in cognisance of Knowledge of Results and or Knowledge of Performance. For example, *reflecting on previous performances we knew to double mark their key player as this would…etc…by applying a man to man strategy immediately would effectively tire them out and give us an advantage… etc…reflecting on my previous results I had to decide which solo piece to execute that would attract the best marks from the judges, etc.*

Consideration of activity challenges and qualities demanded

The responses will be wide ranging and relevant to the activity selected. Candidates should demonstrate acquired Knowledge and Understanding in respect of the specific challenges of the activity selected and importantly demonstrate critical thinking by exemplifying the qualities required as a performer to meet the challenges highlighted.

Reference to the type of activity may be evident to set the scene, for example, an individual/team activity, an indoor/outdoor activity, playing competitively or as leisure pursuit will help qualify the candidate's explanations. For example, in relation to activity challenges,…*in squash the challenges I face are demanding…the aim of the game is to get in to the lead with 9 points over my opponent…a win = best out of three games…the challenges requires me to play the ball against at least one wall away from my opponent to gain points without obstructing my opponents route to ball…The qualities I require are skill related – with high levels of agility and reaction time as I…etc. I require high levels of mental skills to ensure I make tactical decisions, patience being crucial as I outmanoeuvre my opponent to take point advantage…*

(c) *A good response should include some or most of the points as outlined below. Candidates may answer in a detailed manner by targeting limited number of areas within physical, technical, personal and special, or they may approach in a broader manner.*

Qualities: In relation to any of the qualities selected a detailed personal description should be offered. In this respect the candidates may elect to answer from the viewpoint of having a positive or negative affect on performance. Similarly the description could be offered via a synopsis of strengths and weaknesses OR strengths only OR a comparative synopsis via a model performer.
For example, candidates may demonstrate acquired Knowledge and Understanding in respect of the:

Technical Qualities: Reference may be made to wide repertoire of skills eg; *my dribbling, passing shooting etc is consistent and accurate; this may be accompanied by clarification of success rate/quality of execution of PAR. For example, like a model performer I execute my…with power etc.* Reference may also be made to the classification of skills demanded, for example, simple/complex etc.

Physical Qualities: Reference may be made to more than one aspect of fitness. To support acquired/applied Knowledge and Understanding the candidates must describe how the selected aspect of fitness affected performance. For example, *my high levels of Cardio Respiratory Endurance, Speed Endurance helped me maintain pace and track my opponents continuously…etc…my poor flexibility makes it difficult for me to…Unlike a Model Performer my lack of power meant that…etc.*

Personal Qualities: Reference may be made to inherent qualities, for example, *height – helped me to win rebounds consistently, Other acceptable personal qualities such as being* *decisive/determined/confident/competitive etc, put me at an advantage and intimidated my opponents…etc.*

Special Qualities: Reference may be made to the ability to create opportunity, disguise intent, make performance look more dynamic, apply flair, had the ability to choreograph routines/link complex skills… etc. For example, *these unique qualities helped me to fake my intent and so wrong foot my opponent/my routine was exciting to watch…OR this helped me gain more points etc.*

(d) *A good response should include some or most of the points as outlined below. Programme of work must link to the selected quality. Detailed discussion on how the programme helped improve overall performance should form basis of answer. Examples should be used to support argument and illustrate points. The candidate may select an isolated or an integrated training approach.*

Course of action: A good response will include adequate details relevant to the selection and appropriateness of the **MOST** relevant methods of practice/development/training available. Considerations of different methods will be evident in the process. Examples relevant to selected methods and how this will bring about improvement more commensurate to model performer must be evident. For example, *to make sure my lay up shot was more like a model performer. At first I used many repetition drills in a closed environment to ensure I had no pressure…etc. I then progressed to more open practice and used combination/conditioned drills to ensure refinement of shot ie against opposition I was more efficient, accurate.*

A link to other relevant factors may include; whole part whole, gradual build up, problem solving contexts etc.
A good response may typically include other relevant factors to demonstrate Knowledge and Understanding such as, progression, feedback, target setting, work to rest considerations, stages of learning, complexity of technique being developed, factors affecting performance, principles of effective practice.

Planning implications: The candidate's experiences will dictate the terms of reference used, ie as an individual/team game performer or as an athlete or swimmer's perspective some of the following training terms will most commonly be used; short/long term targets, preseason, competitive season and post season, mini, macro, meso cycles, to train in or out with the activity, the need to ensure peak fitness readiness, periodisation principles.

A good response will demonstrate both acquired and applied Knowledge and Understanding. The candidate must reflect on decisions made about their specific training considerations. In this respect, the link to their identified fitness needs will be highlighted with exemplification of the particular stages of training and types of training used. To ensure training effectiveness related Knowledge and Understanding about training principles/principles of effective practice will most likely be made.

Organising of training: Within the response examples should include:
Cognisance of previously stated Strengths & Weaknesses.
Setting of objectives/preparation for competitive event.

Decisions taken as a result of the performance weaknesses/strengths reflective of appropriate training/development method(s) and or selected training regimes.
Training considerations offered should reflect and offer examples based on the: complexity of identified weaknesses, stage of learning, complexity of task etc.

Training considerations may include some or more of the following: training in/out of the activity/conditioning approach, integrated training.

The importance of integrated training: Typically the notion of more than one type of fitness/demand being developed at the same time. Reasons should be included to exhibit related Knowledge and Understanding.

The training programme offered may reflect the development of a technical and skill related quality/demand being developed (or any other relevant combinations). For example, in badminton: the aim = to develop the drop shot WHILST developing improved footwork (agility). The response should include relevant facts; train in the activity using repetition drills − moving to take feeds from right & left hand side of court − combine with footwork drill, eg from T to various numbered areas of court…Progress to combination/conditioned rallies to ensure refinement of shot ie efficiency, accuracy and disguised placement as a result of energy efficient movement to meet the shot with balance and poise to execute the shot and return to base ready for the next shot etc.
A good response will typically include other relevant factors to demonstrate Knowledge and Understanding such as, progression, model performers, feedback, target setting, work to rest considerations, stages of learning, complexity of technique being developed, factors affecting performance, principles of training and or effective practice.

PREPARATION OF THE BODY

3. (a) *A good response should include some or most of the points as outlined below. The candidate must demonstrate acquired knowledge when discussing the different approaches to training. They may focus on one activity; consider several activities; or apply KU in a generic manner.*

Specific training types: A good response should have good description of the form of training for selected approach.
In the activity (conditioning) − fartlek short sprints and then continuous paced running with specific description of what they did. For example, *in athletics for 800 metre running I did fartlek training…did 8 laps…jogged the straights and ran the bends…done without stopping…then did 6 short 60 metre sprints with a short 20 metre jog leading into each sprint made demand similar to end of actual race.*
Out with activity could include circuit training/weight training with description of what they did/sets/reps/types of exercise. For example, *to improve my Cardio Respiratory Endurance for my role as a midfielder in hockey…I trained out with activity…carried out some circuit training…doing high intensity work…work rest ratio 1:3…doing a series of exercises…step ups…burpees…continuous running…3 sets of exercises…working on each for 45 seconds.*
Combination of both: continuous training in pool/weight training out of pool with appropriate description of each/involve some of the following methods fartlek/continuous/conditioning/interval/circuit/weight training/relaxation/breathing/rehearsal. For example, *in swimming I trained using a combination of training within activity and out with activity…within I used interval training…working on developing both anaerobic and aerobic fitness…did warm up…then stroke improvement…main set 6×50 metre swim one minute recovery…sub set 6×50…45 secs recovery…then warm down…out with pool did a weight training circuit…doing a series of exercises…3 sets of exercises…also some work on stepping machines…rowing machines…to improve Cardio Respiratory Endurance.*

Appropriateness of selected method
Within activity: can involve specific movements and can develop skills as well as fitness − involve demands of the activity − can also simulate the pressure demands of a competitive situation − can also be fun and motivational.
Out-with activity: can develop both general and specific muscle/fitness − easy to do − minimum of equipment needed.
Combination: some of the above reasons but firmly explained why − variety in different methods − motivational − enjoyable.

(b) *A good response should include some or most of the points as outlined below. The candidate must demonstrate KU related to both planning and implementing training.*

The importance of planning and implementing training:
Planning could refer to type of activity or level of fitness or role in activity. Goal setting may be referred to types of training may also be referred to for example circuit, interval etc. For example, *I set myself both short term and long term goals...this gave me a target to work towards...they had to be realistic and achievable...they motivated me to do well.*
The answer could refer to the principles of training. Some of the following principles may be referred to − specificity to activity/person/performance − progressive overload − frequency − intensity − duration − adaptation − rest/recovery/over training/reversibility.
You will probably have detail or description of how they were applied to programme and also explanation and justification why they were considered.

(c) *A good response should include some or most of the points as outlined below. Candidates are expected to select one training session from their programme and give a very detailed description. The session described may be very specific to one aspect of fitness or be more general in nature.*

The candidates responses will be wide ranging and depend on the choice of activity and the type or aspect of fitness selected.
For example, *I used interval training for swimming...warm up of 8 lengths multi stroke...then some stroke improvement...then main set...6×50 metre swim with a minute rest between each set...then sub set...6×50...45 sec recovery. This was appropriate because it enables high intensity work combined with rest to allow me to train for a longer period of time and thus gaining greater benefits from training. This was a session to improve speed endurance.*

(d) *A good response should include some or most of the points as outlined below. Candidates should explain in detail how progress was monitored during the training programme.*

The importance of planning and monitoring training using particular methods
Methods used could include video, observation schedules/training diary/logbook, personal evaluation or game analysis.
For example, *I used a training diary...this allowed me to keep a note of my progress...allowed me to see whether my training had been effective...if I had achieved my short term goals...if my training had been set at the correct level...to see if my overall performance had improved.*

4. (a) *A good response should include some or most of the points as outlined below. The candidate must demonstrate KU of each of the types of fitness in relation to their chosen activity.*

Physical skill related and mental types of fitness: You would expect the candidate to select the most appropriate type or more than one aspect within that type to show relevant Knowledge and Understanding to support the answer.

Physical fitness: Cardio Respiratory Endurance − speed − muscular endurance − flexibility − stamina − strength − aerobic/anaerobic endurance − speed endurance − power.

Skill related fitness: reaction time − agility − co-ordination − balance − timing − movement anticipation.

Mental fitness: level of arousal − rehearsal − managing emotion − visualisation − motivation − determination − anxiety/managing stress/ concentration.
All responses should make reference to how the types or aspect(s) chosen relate to **effective** performance in the activity.

Physical fitness: For example, *in football a high level of Cardio Respiratory Endurance and speed endurance allowed me to track and help my defence out...as well as support the attackers...throughout the whole game...also having good strength as a defender allowed me to jump and challenge for high balls and crosses...and win tackles against the opposition.*

Skill related fitness: For example, *in badminton having good agility will allow me quick movement...to reach the shuttle or change direction if necessary and return the shuttle to put my opponent under pressure − also...good timing will allow me to connect with the shuttle in the correct place and allow me to execute the shot correctly...hopefully leading to a successful outcome.*

Mental fitness: For example, *in basketball as the ball carrier by managing my emotions I was able to handle the pressure my opponent was putting on me when closely marking... I was able to make the correct decision and carry out the correct pass to my team mate successfully...when I was also taking a free throw by managing my emotions and rehearsing my routine in my mind...I was able to execute the free throw successfully.*

Relationship between types/aspects of fitness and the development of activity specific fitness
You would expect the candidate to select an appropriate type/aspect of fitness and relate it to the activity selected and show the appropriateness to it.
For example, *in tennis strength and endurance are important...when serving major muscle groups are involved...to produce a strong service action...it is often repeated during a long game...this requires both muscular endurance and strength...this is specific to this movement in tennis.*

(b) *A good response should include some or most of the points as outlined below. The candidate's response should be a detailed description of **one** method.*
The use of video in conjunction with eg an observation schedule can be considered as one of the methods of gathering information. The method selected may be from within or out with activity.

Accurate collection and recording of data
Gathering data: The description of the method could be within the activity. A diagram may feature in the answer for example a time related observation schedule within football showing information relevant to the particular aspect selected which was speed and/Cardio Respiratory Endurance. In the answer the candidate should make reference to the process as to how the information was gathered. A narrative account of what was done and **why** should be obvious showing logical thinking. Methods could

include video/performance profiles/checklists/scatter grams/Preparation, Action, Recovery/stroke counts/breath counts/pulse counts/feedback – reliability and validity of method should be apparent. Methods could come from out with activity. For example, Standardised tests will also be described, these could include:

Physical: 12 minute Cooper test, Sit and reach test, Harvard step test, Bleep test

Skill related: Illinois agility test, Ruler drop, Alternate hand throw

Mental: Questionnaires or self evaluation tests, internal/external feedback

(c) *A good response should include some or most of the points as outlined below. Candidates should demonstrate KU of both validity and reliability in relation to their chosen activity and method.*

Appropriateness of methods used

The appropriateness of the methods described should enable either qualitative or quantative information to be gathered. Explanations offered may include, to provide evidence to compare progress/targets/improvements, to provide a permanent record, can be used time and time again, aids motivation, ensures further challenge and progress, information can be gathered at the beginning and end etc, if video is used it can refer to ability to pause, rewind, play over and over again or be used in conjunction with an observation schedule. For standard tests it allows comparison to set national norms for interpretation.

(d) *A good response should include some or most of the points as outlined below. The candidates response should display both acquired and applied KU when discussing the appropriateness of the selected method of training.*

Appropriate methods of training to improve physical/skill related and mental fitness

The candidates response will be wide ranging and depend on the choice of activity and the type or aspect of fitness selected. Various methods of training could be chosen and some candidates may choose a one session or a block of time to describe what they did. Training could be within activity/out with/combination and involve some of the following methods fartlek/continuous/conditioning/interval/circuit/weight training/relaxation/breathing/rehearsal.

A good response should have good description of the form of training.

In the activity (conditioning): fartlek short sprints and then continuous paced running with specific description of what they did. For example, *in athletics for 800 metre running I did fartlek training...did 8 laps...jogged the straights and ran the bends...done without stopping...then did 6 short 60 metre sprints with a short 20 metre jog leading into each sprint made demand similar to end of actual race.*

Out with activity could include circuit training/weight training with description of what they did/sets/reps/types of exercise. For example, *to improve my Cardio Respiratory Endurance for my role as a midfielder in hockey...I trained out with activity...carried out some circuit training...doing high intensity work...work rest ratio 1:3...doing a series of exercises...step ups...burpees...continuous running...3 sets of exercises... working on each for 45 seconds.*

Combination of both: continuous training in pool/weight training out of pool with appropriate description of each/involve some of the following methods fartlek/continuous/conditioning/interval/circuit/weight training/relaxation/breathing/rehearsal. For example, *in swimming I trained using a combination of training within activity and out with activity...within I used interval training...working on developing both anaerobic and aerobic fitness...did warm up...then stroke improvement...main set 6×50 metre swim one minute recovery...sub set 6×50...45 secs recovery...then warm down...out with pool did a weight training circuit...doing a series of exercises...3 sets of exercises...also some work on stepping machines...rowing machines...to improve Cardio Respiratory Endurance.*

Appropriateness of selected method

Within activity: can involve specific movements and can develop skills as well as fitness – involve demands of the activity – can also simulate the pressure demands of a competitive situation – can also be fun and motivational.

Out-with activity: can develop both general and specific muscle/fitness – easy to do – minimum of equipment needed.

Combination: some of the above reasons but firmly explained why – variety in different methods – motivational – enjoyable.

SKILLS & TECHNIQUES

5. (a) *A good response should include some or most of the points as outlined below.*

Information Processing

Relevant description; this may be supported with use of a diagram. The description should include details appropriate to the skill/technique selected.

The 4 stages should appear in sequence order of INPUT via stimuli/senses/instruction/demonstration or feedback offered. DECISION MAKING – action to be taken. OUTPUT via taking appropriate action.

EVALUATION – what was the outcome of action taken; successful/unsuccessful, effective/ineffective.

Remediation process now occurs – repeat the action to develop/refine – regress to address weaknesses identified – progress to the next stage.

Skill classification

Relevant description of various types of skill. The description should include details appropriate to the skills selected inclusive of example. The classified skills likely to appear: Open/Closed. Discrete/Serial/Continuous. Simple/Complex.

Points highlighted:

Open – dependent on different variables, externally paced eg a corner kick in football.

Closed – Internally paced, no clear beginning or ending, eg a drive in golf.

Discrete – clear beginning and end, requiring fine motor skills.

Serial – a combination of discrete skills which performed in sequence produces a unique skill such as lay up in Basketball.

Continuous – no clear pattern of beginning or end such as swimming.

Simple – requiring few sub routines, no element of danger = forward roll in gymnastics.

Complex – many sub routines, element of danger = front somersault in gymnastics.

(b) *A good response should include some or most of the points as outlined below.*

Features of a skilled performance

A good response will include reference to the range and qualities that are evident in a skilled/model performance. Reference should be made across the range of qualities displayed ie technical, physical, skill and mental related. A link to other relevant factors may include; wide repertoire of skills evident and executed at the correct time with consistency, fluency, ease of economy. Movements/application of skills seem effortless. Management of emotions are controlled. A degree of confidence. Few unforced errors. Makes appropriate decisions when under pressure etc.

(c) *A good response should include some or most of the points as outlined below. More than 1 method of practice must be mentioned in the programme of work.*

Programme of work: The responses offered will be wide ranging and will depend on the candidate's choice of skill/technique identified for development.

The response may include details of the considerations/critical debate about the selection and appropriateness of the methods of practice/development programme followed. In this respect the candidate should be convincing in their argument about why one method was selected in preference to another ie the 'process' should be obvious and justified.

Programme references may include details of weeks 1 & 2, weeks 3 & 4, weeks 5 & 6, etc OR *I used a gradual build up/whole part whole approach to my development programme.* In this respect the notion of reliability/validity should be apparent and justified etc.

The content and structure given may be justified with progressions exemplified to demonstrate sound Knowledge and Understanding. For example, *as I was at the cognitive stage – I used many shadow/repetition practices to ensure…etc. At the associative stage I used some shadow/repetition practices progressing to combination drills…etc. At the automatic stage of learning I knew to use more pressure/problem solving drills as these would challenge me more…etc. I found the skill very difficult so decided to use gradual build up as this would…etc…In weeks 1 & 2, I concentrated more on simple drills…in weeks 3-4, I progressed to more complex drills such as…etc this built my confidence as I reached my target of…etc.* A link to other relevant factors may include; whole part, gradual build up, mass/distributed, closed/open contexts, repetitions, target setting, model performers etc.

(d) *A good response should include some or most of the points as outlined below.*

The importance of monitoring and reviewing: A good response will highlight the differences/benefits of the purpose of monitoring = ie the ongoing process. Such as – reference to appropriate data methods to facilitate comparison of improvements, achieving targets set, gaining and acting on feedback, aids motivation, ensures further challenge and progress.

Importantly, the response must include reference to reviewing performance = ie summative progress.

Many candidates will repeat or include some of the previously mentioned comments. However reference to the evaluation of the whole process ie the impact of the training/development programme/programme of work should be highlighted. Judgements on the success/effectiveness of the programme/used PLUS judgements on the success/ effectiveness to whole performance must be clearly defined.

A good response will highlight the impact of skill technique development to WHOLE performance development. For example, *a more consistent application/less errors/more points won, a positive benefit including greater confidence etc.*

6. (a) *A good response should include some or most of the points as outlined below.*

Stages of learning: A good response will include specific reference and detail appropriate with detailed explanations relevant to the stage of learning described. Examples are often included to highlight their understanding in context; this may be generic or linked to a specific skill/technique.

For example, at the cognitive stage a performer will be reliant on a lot of instruction/feedback. The performer is learning about the sub routines of the skill/technique. Success rate/effectiveness is not refined etc.

At the associative stage, a performer will still be reliant on instruction/feedback but will be developing ability to self evaluate. The performer is more able to link the sub routines of the skill/technique; the execution of the skill is recognisable but the success rate/effectiveness is still not consistent or highly effective etc.

At the automatic stage, a performer will be less reliant on instruction/feedback with an ability to self evaluate and identify weaknesses. The performer is able to link the sub routines of the skill/technique; the execution of the skill is recognisable with control and consistency etc.

A link to other relevant factors may include; progressions possible from one stage to the next, model/skilled performer etc.

(b) *A good response should include some or most of the points as outlined below.*

Programme of work: The responses offered will be wide ranging and will depend on the candidate's choice of skill/technique identified for development.

The response must include details of the considerations/critical debate about the selection and appropriateness of the methods of practice/development programme followed. In this respect the candidate should be convincing in their argument about why one method was selected in preference to another ie the 'process' should be obvious and justified.

The programme followed should be detailed with reference made to the stage of learning and some of the following considerations: skill complexity classification, Model Performer, feedback, goal setting…etc.

For example, at the cognitive stage – many shadow/repetition practices were incorporated to ensure…etc.
At the associative stage some shadow/repetition practices progressing to combination drills, etc. At the automatic stage of learning more pressure/ problem solving drills were used to advance and challenge learning and performance development.
A link to other relevant factors may include; whole part, gradual build up, mass/distributed, closed/open contexts etc.

(c) *A good response should include some or most of the points as outlined below.*

Motivation/Concentration/Feedback
In this respect the candidate may give a detailed synopsis of how each factor selected impacted upon their learning and or their application of skill/technique. Merit should be given according to depth/quality/relevance of explanations offered.
NOTE – it is likely that similar points may be referenced/exemplified in relation to discrete factor.

Motivation = A good response will include details of being internally (intrinsic)/externally (extrinsic) motivated to learn/achieve success. Being motivated enables the performer to be self driven to listen to instruction and act on it, it helps the performer to be self determined/give off their best/come from behind/respond to immediate problems/competitive challenges/not worry if mistakes are made and re channel focus.

Concentration = A good response will include details of the need to concentrate/focus on instruction/demonstration offered to ensure effective execution/application of skill or technique, promotes progression/adaptation of skill or technique, ensures bad habits are not formed/eradicated, enables the performer to perform their role and apply their skills appropriately, promotes the ability to read play/make effective decisions/adapt to the immediate situation…etc. In the context of games, concentration enables the performer to stick to role related duties/application of structure/strategy/game plan…etc.

Feedback = A good response will include details of receiving internal (kinaesthetic) feedback to progress/refine skill or technique OR receiving/giving external feedback (visual/verbal/written/vestibular), to progress/refine skill or technique of self or that of others.
Feedback should be positive/immediate to promote confidence/success.

NOTE A link to Stage of Learning, Model Performers may be made in reference to any of the above factors.

(d) *A good response should include some or most of the points as outlined below.*

Whole performance development
The responses offered will be wide ranging however a good response will highlight the impact of improved skill/technique development to WHOLE performance effectiveness. For example a more consistent application/less errors/more points won, a positive benefit including greater confidence etc.

The candidate may also include details referencing specific drills or parts of the programme that benefited their performance, for example, *I felt that the repetition drills such as…improved my ability to etc.* Similarly a comparative synopis via a statistical % comparison before & after, or comparative to a Model Performer may also feature in the response.

Merit should be given to the feasibility/validity/justification for claims of improved performance.

STRUCTURES, STRATEGIES AND COMPOSITION

7. (a) *A good response should include some or most of the points as outlined below.*

Select a relevant structure, strategy or composition
The candidate must describe the Structure, Strategy or Composition. Some will also make reference possibly to the role they played as well.
These will include fast break/zones/1-3-1/horse shoe offence in basketball/man/man defence
Football – 4-2-4/4-3-3/3-5-2
Badminton – front-back-side-side
Gymnastics particular sequence – routine
Tennis – serve-volley
Volleyball – rotation
Hockey – penalty corner

For example, *in tennis I used a serve volley strategy – I would serve fast and hard to opponent – follow my serve – get into net and position quickly – use a volley to win point – from opponents return.*

(b) *A good response should include some or most of the points as outlined below.*

Structure and strategy fundamentals
The following may be referred to or listed.
Using space in attack and defence, pressuring opponents, tempo of play, speed in attack, delay in defence and principles of play (width, depth and mobility).
The importance should be justified and show both acquired and applied knowledge.
For example, *in basketball I wanted to play a fast tempo game…attack quickly…so I made sure that on each opportunity we tried to play a fast break…to catch the defence out…score a quick basket…create an overload situation…before the defence was organised properly.*

Structure and compositional fundamentals
The following may be referred to or listed.
Design form, developing motifs, using repetition, variation and contrast, interpreting stimulus in developing performance, using space effectively, using creativity in performance.
The importance should be justified and show both acquired and applied knowledge.
For example, *in dance I started with a simple step motif…took me forwards then back to starting position…then sideways…back to starting…I established this as a simple core motif…then I developed a second core motif…this time a jumping pattern…then I began to mix and play with both core motifs…to add interest to my dance…gave my dance variety and quality of movement contrasts.*

(c) *A good response should include some or most of the points as outlined below.*
The responses will be wide ranging and will depend on the choice of structure, strategy or composition selected.
Responses should start with a description of the problem they faced.
For example, *opposition had good outside shooters…scored frequently…we found when attacking all 4 players in midfield would be up the park…supporting the forwards…when the attack broke down the opposition often broke quickly…our midfield were slow to get back…our defence was under pressure.*

(d) *A good response should include some or most of the points as outlined below. Answer should demonstrate critical thinking and decision making in the justification of any changes/adaptations or in the training programme which was organised to overcome the problems faced.*

The importance of adapting and refining a structure, strategy or composition in response to performance demands
The responses will be wide ranging and will depend on the choice of structure, strategy or composition selected.
Responses may repeat the description of the problem they faced. They should then show evidence of problem solving and decision making to make their performance more effective. The candidate may decide to change structure, strategy or composition completely. For example, *in basketball we were playing a 2-1-2 zone…opposition had good outside shooters…scored frequently…we changed to half court man/man defence to stop them…this led to less successful shots as they were under more pressure…forced them to try and drive to basket. They made more mistakes…scored less baskets as they were poor at driving to basket…we won more turnovers and could attack more.*

8. *(a)* (i) *A good response should include some or most of the points as outlined below.*

Some candidates may answer by referring to the strengths as a team or strengths of the individual.

For example...*in tennis I used a serve, volley strategy. As I had a consistent, fast first serve, I would serve fast and hard to my opponent, follow my serve into the net, positioning quickly in order to capitalise on my opponent's weak return.*

An explanation of the impact of this strength on the whole performance must be given, for example, *My strength allowed me to dictate the rally from the first stroke. I took control of the front court area, dominating the court, putting my opponent under pressure immediately, inevitably winning many points easily in my service game.*

(ii) *A good response should include some or most of the points as outlined below.*

Some candidates may answer by referring to the strengths as a team or strengths of the individual.

Candidates must show critical thinking by offering a degree of authenticity in their analysis and must make reference as to how their WHOLE performance was affected by the weakness, for example...

My backhand volley was poor – made most errors from this technique – usually went into net or out of court – lost many points – poor second serve – often too short – opponents exploit this leading to lost points – exploitation by opponent – passed on many occasions. (Also a link to other factors such as reduced confidence, lack of fitness etc may be evident in answers).

(b) A good response should include some or most of the points as outlined below.

Weakness addressed: The responses offered will be wide ranging and will depend on the choice of SSTC selected and the weakness(es) identified. The responses could be a description of the programme of work followed but this must be relevant to weakness mentioned. For example, *for my backhand volley I carried out a skill development programme...partner threw me a ball...play a backhand volley...gradually increased speed and distance...added more pressure...eventually to full speed...then aim for targets on court...two feeders drive me the ball from back of court...alternative backhand/forehand volley...serve to partner and get them to return to backhand side to play volley.* Various methods of training/practice may be described – reference may be made to possible changes to SSTC either as individuals or as part of a team...a range of development programmes will be evident – the structure should be evident as well as the content – the SSTC may be changed or adapted to overcome weakness(es)...substitute player. Responses must show critical thinking and relevant decision making and should reduce the effect of weakness(es) on performance.

(c) A good response should include some or most of the points as outlined below.

The responses will include descriptions of particular methods to gather information on effectiveness followed by an explanation – these could include video-game analysis – observation schedules – knowledge of results – criteria checklists – statistics – personal reflection - feedback – internal/external – comparison to previous information gathered - match analysis sheets. For example, *in basketball...we used a criteria checklist...all aspects of fast break...data was collected from a game this then allowed... ...comparison to previous...to see if we had improved its effectiveness.*

(d) A good response should include some or most of the points as outlined below.

Structure and strategy fundamentals
Using space in attack and defence, pressuring opponents, tempo of play, speed in attack, delay in defence and principles of play (width, depth and mobility).
The importance should be justified and show both acquired and applied knowledge.
For example, *in basketball I wanted to play a fast tempo game...attack quickly...so I made sure that on each opportunity we tried to play a fast break...to catch the defence out...score a quick basket...create an overload situation...before the defence was organised properly.*

Structure and compositional fundamentals
Design form, developing motifs, using repetition, variation and contrast, interpreting stimulus in developing performance, using space effectively, using creativity in performance.
The importance should be justified and show both acquired and applied knowledge.
For example, *in dance I started with a simple step motif...took me forwards then back to starting position...then sideways...back to starting...I established this as a simple core motif...then I developed a second motif...this time a jumping pattern...then I began to mix and play with both core motifs...to add interest to my dance...gave my dance variety and quality of movement contrasts.*

HIGHER PHYSICAL EDUCATION
2011

In the Higher Physical Education examination candidates will have answered from the perspective of their experiences in a wide variety of activities. To produce an activity specific marking scheme would result in an enormous document which would be extremely cumbersome and time-consuming to use and which could never realistically cover all possibilities.

In relation to **all** questions it should be noted that the relevance of the content in the candidates' responses will depend on:

- the activity selected
- the performance focus
- the training/development programme/programme of work selected
- the practical experiences of their course as the contexts for answers.

AREA 1 – PERFORMANCE APPRECIATION

1. (a) **Model Performance**
    The response may focus on the student's strengths and weaknesses in comparison to model performance.

    Reference could be made to a range of qualities:
    - Technical
    - Physical
    - Personal
    - Special

    For example, *unlike a model performer I do not have a repertoire of skills to meet the technical demands…I fail to execute my…at the correct time and lack consistency, fluency. Unlike the model performer I took clumsy and lack economy of movement…they make everything look effortless…their movements/application of skills are used at the right time. However, like the model performer, I can manage my emotions… I rarely display bad temper and concentrate fully on my game/role.*

    (b) **Performance qualities**
    The student should select **ONE** quality. The response should focus on how components of this quality were improved over a number of sessions.

    It is important that the student is able to describe the actual programme of work used to improve the selected quality.

    For example…*to develop my technical ability in badminton I initially worked on my overhead clear and my net shot in isolation…I did this by using feeder practices…I focused on my movement to the shot and my recovery back to base…I then moved to make use of pressure drills and conditioned games…*

    (c) **Performance Strengths**
    The response should focus on how strengths within the selected quality were utilised in whole performance.

    For example…*physical quality…in football…Being powerful enabled me to win more headers and compete in tackles…being strong helped me hold off defenders when I was in possession of the ball…being fast enabled me to run into space to receive a pass.*

    (d) **Evaluating performance**
    The response should focus on reviewing as a summative process. Reference should be made to some of the following:
    - Achieving goals
    - Motivational effects
    - Setting new targets
    - Appropriateness of course of action
    - Success of training programme
    - Comparing whole performance before and after training

    For example…*I compared my performance when playing badminton before to training to see if I had improved the effectiveness and consistency (technical qualities) of my overhead shots in the game.*

    The response must also focus on giving a clear description of method(s) used to evaluate overall performance following programme of work.

    For example…*match analysis, video of whole performance.*

2. (a) **Nature of performance**
    The response should focus on the following:
    - Individual/team
    - Duration of event
    - Number of participants
    - Environment (indoor/outdoor)
    - Directly/indirectly competitive
    - Scoring system
    - Rules
    - Codes of conduct
    - Spectators/audience

    For example…*in a tennis game there can be 2 players (single) or 4 players (doubles)…a game can last 3 sets or 5 sets. A women's game last for 3 sets. The winner is the person who is the first to achieve 2 sets…the winner of the set has to win by more than one game…if a set is tied at 6 all…a tie break follows…*

    (b) **Mental preparation**
    The response should give a clear description of how the performer prepared mentally for performance.

    Reference may be made to the following.
    - Deep breathing
    - Mental rehearsal
    - Visualisation
    - Trigger words
    - Meditation
    - Self talk

    For example…*to enable me to control my anxiety prior to performing my gymnastics routine…I used visualisation to picture myself completing my floor routine successfully…this let me see myself going through all the parts…linking together…landing securely.*

    (c) **Integrated training**
    The response should describe in detail an integrated programme that developed a variety of the following aspects:
    - Physical (preparation of the body)
    - Technical (skills and techniques)
    - Personal (motivation and personal goals)
    - Special (achieving peak performance)
    - Mental (rehearsal, imagery, visualisation)
    - Strategic/compositional planning (structures, strategies and composition)

    For example…*in badminton I wanted to develop the drop shot while improving my footwork (agility)…I trained in the activity using repetition drills to improve my drop shot…I also combined this with specific agility drills to improve my footwork.*

    (d) **Whole performance improvements**
    The response should include discussion and evaluative comments on how student's overall performance was improved.

    It would be expected the student would give examples of improvements made as a result of training.

    For example…*Working on my deep breathing helped me to stay calm and avoid distractions around the poolside before the race started. This helped me get a good start…the work I carried out on my tumble turn technique made my turn smoother, more powerful and shallower. This resulted in...the programme enabled me to...as a result my performance...*

AREA 2 – PREPARATION OF THE BODY

3. (a) Information gathering

The response must show evidence of the importance of gathering evidence about the student's fitness.

Reference should be made to some of the following:
- Starting point for training
- Goal/target setting
- Needs are identified
- Comparisons before and after training possible
- Identifying strengths and weaknesses in relations to types of fitness required for activity
- Comparison with national norms

For example...*I need to know what my base level of fitness was before I started training...this lets me identify my training load before I begin my programme.*

(b) Phases of training

The response must show evidence of acquired knowledge of the phases of training. Reference must be made to each of the following phases:
- Pre season
- Competition
- Transition/close season

For example...*before the hockey season starts I know I have to build up my aerobic fitness so that I have gained a sound base to then move onto more intense, competition phase...in the close season I would return to winding down, keeping my fitness ticking over by general swimming, cycling etc.*

(c) Phases of training – training programme

The response must describe a relevant training programme for the selected phase of training. Reference should be made to some of the following methods of training:
- Continuous running
- Interval running
- Circuits
- Fartlek
- Conditioning
- Weights
- Relaxation, breathing and rehearsal

For example...*in the pre season for football...I carried out a circuit 3 times a week...I did various sets of repetitions and exercises designed to build up my aerobic fitness...these included step ups, sit ups, shuttle runs, squat jumps...*

In the competition phase I used plyometrics to build up the power in my legs for jumping to head the ball...I also worked on set plays such as corner kicks to allow me to practice jumping under pressure in a competition situation.

In post season I did some gentle cycling and swimming to allow some rest and recovery and keep my fitness ticking over...

(d) Goal setting

The response should show evidence of the factors considered when setting goals. The student should also provide examples of the goals they set. Reference should be made to the following:
- The point in the season
- Current level of performance
- Competition phases
- Appropriateness of chosen goals eg achievable and realistic
- The use of goals to enhance motivation
- The ability to monitor progress towards achieving goals
- Types of goals eg short or long term

For example...*I set myself a short term goal for swimming was to improve my time for the 50metres front crawl over a period of a month by 1 second...this gave me a realistic target to work towards and motivated me to work hard and stay focused when training...another goal I set was to improve the strength for the arm action in the front crawl...this would enable me to have a more efficient pull through the water...leading to an improved time for my overall swim...this would be a long term target...*

4. (a) Mental aspects of fitness

The response should focus on explaining the aspects of mental fitness. Reference should be made to some of the following:
- Level of arousal
- Mental rehearsal
- Managing emotions
- Visualisation
- Managing stress/pressure
- Concentration
- Determination
- Motivation

For example...*in basketball as the ball carrier, I was able to handle the pressure my opponent put on me...I also was able to manage my emotions when my opponent appeared to foul me and the referee did not award a foul...this ensured I did not pick up a technical foul by reacting to this decision.*

(b) Skill and physical aspects of fitness

The response should include detailed description of relevant aspects of physical and skill related aspects of fitness in relation to the selected activity. Reference may be made to the following:
- Physical
- Speed
- Strength
- Power
- Flexibility
- Cardio respiratory endurance
- Speed endurance
- LME

For example...*high level of CRE allowed me to track and help out my defence as well as supporting attackers throughout the whole game...having good strength allowed me to jump and challenge for high balls and crosses.*

Skill Related
- Reaction time
- Agility
- Balance
- Timing
- Coordination
- Movement anticipation

For example...*in badminton, good agility allows me quick movement to reach the shuttle or change direction quickly...good timing enables me to connect with the shuttle in the correct place allowing me to execute the shot correctly.*

(c) Principles of training

The response should show acquired knowledge of the principles of training considered when planning a fitness training programme. Reference should be made to the following:
- Specificity – activity, personal and aspect of fitness
- Overload – frequency, intensity and duration
- Progression
- Rest and recovery
- Reversibility
- Adaptation

For example…*I made sure the training was specific to the weakness identified…also to the demands of the activity…I trained 3 times per week with rest every other day…this allows my body to recover*

(d) Adaptation to training programme

The response must refer as to why changes were made to the student's training programme. Reference could be made to the following:
- To provide qualitative or quantitative details of the effectiveness of training programme
- To ensure progression and challenge while training
- Correct intensity of training programme
- To ensure motivation stays high while training
- To make sure short term goals are achieved
- To prevent boredom and provide variety
- To return to training after injury or absence from training

For example…*I applied overload after week 3 of my training programme…I did this by increasing the number of sets because I was finding my training too easy and knew I needed to keep forcing my body to adapt and get fitter…this prevented boredom and kept my motivation high.*

AREA 3 – SKILLS AND TECHNIQUES

5. (a) Gathering information on Performance Strengths or Weaknesses

The response should focus on the information generated as a result of:
- Mechanical analysis
- Movement analysis
- Consideration of quality

For example…*when looking at my overhead clear using my PAR sheet (movement analysis), I could see at the preparation phase that I was turning side on…It became obvious to me that my weakness was at the action phase. I was not using a straight arm or hitting the shuttle when it was in front of my body. The transfer of weight was also not happening from my back foot to my front foot. At the recovery phase…*

(b) Appropriate methods of data collection

The response should focus on the appropriateness of the method described. Students must justify why the approach was appropriate. Reference should enable either qualitative or quantitative details of performance progress.

For example…*this provides evidence to compare progress/targets/improvements…a permanent record, can be used time and time again, aids motivation, and ensures further challenge and progress, information can be gathered at the beginning/middle and end etc. When using a video there is the opportunity to benefit from using the pause/rewind facility etc.*

(c) Course of action

The response should focus on the justification of the candidate's chosen course of action.
The response must indicate details of the considerations/critical debate about the selection and appropriateness of the materials of practice/development programme followed. In this respect the candidates should be convincing in their argument about **why** one method was selected in preference to another ie the 'process' should be obvious and justified.

The course of action followed should be detailed with reference to **some** of the following considerations:
- Stages of Learning
- Skill complexity
- Skill classification (open/closed)
- Model Performer
- Feedback

- Goal setting
- Methods of practice

Programme references may include actual description of the work carried out over a period of time.

For example…*As I was at the cognitive stage – I used many shadow/repetition practices to ensure – etc. At the associative stage I used some shadow/repetition practices progressing to combination drills…etc. At the automatic stage of learning I knew to use more pressure/problem solving drills as these would challenge me more…etc. I found the skill very difficult so decided to use gradual build up as this would…etc. In weeks 1&2, I concentrated more on simple drills…in weeks 3-4, I progressed to more complex drills such as…etc this built my confidence as I reached my target of…etc.*

(d) Feedback

The response should focus on the variety of types of feedback available when developing performance.
The student should comment on a combination of methods of feedback such as kinaesthetic, knowledge of results, knowledge of performance, verbal visual or written feedback when developing their performance. Responses must include the importance of using more than one type of feedback in the development process.

For example…*while developing my performance, I used my General observation schedule (written feedback) to identify the weakness in my game…this was useful as it…I then made use of the visual feedback from the video recording (visual feedback)…to see for myself where my volley was letting me down. By using different types of feedback I was able to get a full picture of my strengths and weaknesses, making my data collection more valid and reliable.*

6. (a) Features of a model performance

The response must explain the advantages of considering a model performance. Reference may be made to the following:
- Range of qualities – technical, physical, special and personal
- Example of high quality performance – few unforced errors, good decision making under pressure
- Comparison to own performance – strengths and weaknesses
- Motivation
- Confidence
- Goal setting
- Visual picture

For example…*I used the Model to help me first of all get a picture in my mind's eye of what I was aiming to do…this helped me set targets and stay motivated to work through my training programme.*

(b) Strengths and weaknesses

The response must refer to the student's strengths and weaknesses when applying their selected skill or technique. References could be made to the following:
- Preparation, action, recovery of skill
- Execution of skill
- Consistency in application of skill
- Qualities – technical, physical and practical
- Effectiveness of skill
- Mechanical principles – balance, centre of gravity, levers
- Fluency, control
- Timing

For example…*when performing the lay up in basketball, one of my weaknesses was the footwork… when executing the skill I often took off the wrong foot…this led to me being imbalanced…*

(c) **Principles of effective practices**

The response must show acquired knowledge of the Principles of effective practice. Reference should be made to some of the following:
- Setting clear objective
- Strengths and weaknesses consideration
- Awareness of model performer
- Achievable stages
- Effect of boredom and fatigue
- Intensity of practice
- Work rest ratio

Often the acronym S.M.A.R.T.E.R. features in the candidate's answers

For example...*practice should be specific, measurable, attainable, time related, exciting and regular.
...as my programme was specific it helped me to achieve success...I could target the specific part of my technique that need most improvement. I know to set targets and raise them once...this ensures my practice was motivating etc.*

(d) The response must give description of the method of practice used with relevant explanation as to it's appropriateness. The response offered will be wide ranging and will depend on the candidate's choice of skill/technique identified for development.
The response must include a description of an appropriate method of practice. These could include:

- Shadow practice
- Opposed/unopposed practice
- Gradual build up
- Whole part whole
- Drills
- Repetition
- Conditioned games
- Small sided games

For example...*in badminton I used conditioned games...I played against an opponent where I could win an extra point if I won the rally by using the smash*

The second response must indicate details of the considerations/critical debate about the selection and appropriateness of the methods of practice/development programme followed. In the respect the candidate should be convincing in their argument about why one method was selected in preference to another ie the 'process' should be obvious and justified.

Reference could be made to some of the following considerations:
- Stages of learning
- Skill complexity/skill classification
- Current Ability level
- Difficulty of practice

For example...*The stages of learning...as I was at the cognitive stage – I used many shadow/repetition practices to ensure that I was able to slow the movement down as I was wanting to get the foundations of the skill correct... at the associative stage I used some shadow/repetition practices progressing to combination drills...this made my work a bit more demanding and game like... at the automatic stage of learning I knew to use more pressure/problem solving drills as these would challenge me more...etc.*

AREA 4 – STRUCTURES, STRATEGIES AND COMPOSITIONS

7. (a) **Methods to gather information**

The response should focus on how information was gathered when applying the structure, strategy or composition (SSC). Reference must be made to the description of method(s) used to gather information on the effectiveness of the SSC. These may include video-game analysis-observation schedules-knowledge of results-criteria checklists-statistics-personal reflection-feedback-internal/external-comparison to previous information gathered-match analysis sheets.

For example...*in basketball...we used a criteria checklist...all aspects of fast break...data was collected from a game this then allowed...comparison to previous...to see if we had improved its effectiveness.*

(b) **Recognising the need to maximise strengths within a structure, strategy or composition**

The response should focus on how the student made best use of their strengths when applying their SSC.
The answers may vary according to the Structure, Strategy or Composition selected. The following factors may be apparent in answers-to use particular players with particular roles-strengths of these players-type of opposition-attack/defence being applied by my team or opposition-time restrictions in game-after a particular time or situation in activity-ground/weather conditions-prior or previous knowledge of opponent/s-previous results.

For example...*When playing basketball we used the three tallest players we had to form the rebound triangle in our zone defence so we could collect rebounds defensively when our opposition missed their shots at the basket.*

(c) **Problems encountered**

The response should focus on problems which occurred when applying the selected SSC. The student must give a description of actual problems encountered.
The responses will be wide ranging and will depend on the choice of structure, strategy or composition selected.

For example...*in basketball we were playing a 2-1-2 zone...opposition had good outside shooters ...scored frequently...and as a team we were not working together as a unit...this led to...*

(d) **Decisions taken to develop performance**

The response should focus on how the student justified the course of action taken to develop their performance. Response should show evidence of problem solving and decision making to make their performance more effective.

The candidate may decide to alter the structure, strategy or composition. For example...*in football we played a 4-4-2 formation...we found when attacking all 4 players in midfield would be up the park...supporting the forwards...when the attack broke down the opposition often broke quickly...our midfield were slow to get back...our defence was under pressure...we adapted the structure, strategy or composition by having one player...holding in midfield in front of back four...one midfield supporting strikers...and two in middle to move back and forward as necessary...this led to a more balanced attack and defence and allowed us to prevent the opposition breaking quickly. Holding midfield was able to delay attack...allows others to get back.*

The candidates may decide to follow a programme of work to develop their performance. For example...*in netball...the centre pass strategy was not effective because of ineffective dodging from the Wing Attack...we did some work on feinting without defenders…we gradually added passing…then passive defenders…then active defenders.*

8. (a) **Structure, strategy or composition**

The response must focus on two different SSCs. The candidate must describe **TWO** Structures, Strategy or Composition. Some will also make reference possibly to the role they played as well.

These may include:
Basketball-fast break…zones…1-3-1…horse shoe offence…man/man defence.
Football-4-2-4/4-3-3/3-5-2/3-5-1.
Badminton front-back-side-side.
Gymnastics particular sequence-routine.
Volleyball-Rotational setter, Specialist setter, W service reception formation.
Hockey penalty corner-passing it back to the 'injector' on the post.

For example…*in tennis I used a serve volley strategy-I would serve fast and hard to opponent-follow my serve-get into net and position quickly-use a volley to win point-from opponents return.*

In hockey…I played in a zone defence where I had to cover a particular area of the pitch.

(b) **The advantage of various SSCs**

The responses must focus on one of the selected SSC in part (a). The student must show evidence of the advantage of using this SSC.

For example…*the advantage in football of using a 3-5-2 formation is that it is easier to dominate midfield…can cover wide areas of pitch…has a variety of attack options linking midfield and forwards.*

(c) **The advantage of various SSCs**

The response must focus on one of the selected SSC in part (a). The student must show evidence of the advantage of using this SSC.

For example…*My specialist setter can give me the type of set I prefer to be able to perform an effective spike…she can play a good set from even a poor first pass…giving my team the chance of more attacking plays.*

(d) **Limitations of various SSCs**

The response must focus on ONE limitation of EACH of the selected SSCs.

For example…*Limitations of a 3-5-2 in football is that the defence can be exposed…by long passes…played straight from defence…midfield can be bypassed.*

Volleyball…the limitation of using a specialist setter is that there can be many rotational faults as people move too early before the service is taken or there is confusion in the front court as to who moves where and when.

HIGHER PHYSICAL EDUCATION 2012

In the Higher Physical Education examination candidates will have answered from the perspective of their experiences in a wide variety of activities. To produce an activity specific marking scheme would result in an enormous document which would be extremely cumbersome and time-consuming to use and which could never realistically cover all possibilities.

In relation to **all** questions it should be noted that the relevance of the content in the candidates' responses will depend on:

- the activity selected
- the performance focus
- the training/development programme/programme of work selected
- the practical experiences of their course as the contexts for answers.

PERFORMANCE APPRECIATION

1. (a) **Model Performance/Demands of performance**

The response should consider a range of demands that can be identified through considering models of performance.

Demands could be:
- Technical, physical, personal, special
- Competitive or non-competitive
- Scoring systems
- Roles
- Rules

For example, *watching a model performance allowed me to understand the different roles the players adopted… I could see how the player managed to perform skills with control and accuracy even when they were under pressure from opponents… the players were composed and focused… the power they generated when performing jumps was important to the success of their movements.*

(b) **Physical and technical demands of an activity**

The response should include the key physical and technical demands of the selected activity.

For example… *to perform well in badminton I had to have a repertoire of skills that I could perform with a high degree of accuracy…Net shot enabled me to…, good clears were vital because…I also required a high level of endurance as ….it was very important that I could move around the court quickly, using the correct footwork patterns.*

(c) **Mental factors affecting performance**

The response should include reference to, mental factors to be considered both before and during performance.

- Optimum state of arousal
- Maintaining motivation, confidence and concentration
- Control of aggression
- Anxiety
- Managing emotions

(d) **Planning and managing personal improvement performance**

The response should consider both the planning and managing of a programme.

For example… *I practiced using relaxation techniques in training, this involved….Once I could do this I used this before performances. To improve my ability to control my emotions during a performance I learned to…*

2. (a) **Personal and special qualities**

The response should give a clear description of both the personal and special qualities required. Students may describe one personal and one special quality in depth or may describe a range of personal and special qualities.

Special – imagination, flair, creativity, deception
Personal – desire to succeed, determination, ability to work with others

(b) **Performance improvement programme**

The response should justify the programme implemented in order to improve personal or special qualities.

For example… *to improve our desire to succeed we identified and shared our objectives. To improve our creativity and become less predictable in attacking set pieces we…*

(c) **Evaluating progress**

The response should describe one method of evaluating the success of the programme.

Video, match analysis, questionnaires, etc

NOTE: to use video footage to facilitate another method is acceptable

(d) **Setting short and long term goals**

For example… *It was very important for me to set achievable short term goals with clear success criteria as means of reaching my long term goal…Specific to focus attention…motivational effect when I achieved…kept my training focused…set new goals…recorded for feedback.*

PREPARATION OF THE BODY

3. (a) **Fitness demands**

The response should discuss the fitness requirements of effective performance.

For example… *In Basketball physical fitness is very important because it enables players to…I considered speed to be the most important aspect because…It was also very important that I could change direction quickly and coordinate my movements. This allowed me to…Managing emotions in basketball is also vital because…*

(b) **Whole performance improvements**

The response should describe the impact of the training on the whole performance.

For example… *My physical training programme to develop power had a positive impact on my ability to rebound. This enabled me to make a better contribution to the team by…Improvements to my agility helped me in both attacking and defending situations by…*

(c) **Method(s) of training**

The response should focus on description of the method(s) of training such as circuit; interval; conditioning; rehearsal; continuous. Examples of the work undertaken within a training session or programme should be used to assist in describing the method. Students may answer by describing one method or by describing more than one method.

For example… *To develop my speed endurance the method of training I used sqas interval training. This involved me working for a period of time, having a period of rest, then working again. I sprinted 50m, then rested for 15 seconds. I repeated that 10 times – this represented a work:rest ratio of approximately 1:2. My next set involved running for 200m in a target time of 45 seconds… reps work:rest ratio.*

(d) **Appropriate method(s) of training**

Students may answer by explaining why one, or more than one, method of training was appropriate.

For example… *Conditioning is a very appropriate method of developing cardio-respiratory endurance. We were motivated by the small-sided games and worked hard for the whole time. We developed our team-work and skills at the same time…We were able to keep above our aerobic training threshold for the whole time, this is important because…*

4. (a) **Types of Fitness**

The response should discuss the importance of one type.

Physical fitness – Cardio Respiratory Endurance-speed-muscular endurance-flexibility-stamina-strength-aerobic-anaerobic endurance-speed endurance-power
or
Skill related fitness – reaction time-agility-co-ordination-balance-timing-movement anticipation
or
Mental fitness – level of arousal-rehearsal-managing emotion-visualisation-motivation-determination-anxiety/managing stress/concentration

(b) **Training programme**

The response should give details of the content and the frequency of sessions within the programme. It should also describe how progressive overload was applied.

(c) **Types of fitness**

The response should explain the importance of the two types of fitness not selected in part (a).

(d) **Fitness assessment**

For example… *Assessing my fitness prior to starting my training programme allowed me to see where my weaknesses were in my actual performance…identify the type(s) and aspect(s) of fitness I should be trying to develop…Fitness tests gave me objective results which I could use as my baseline…I could make my training at the correct level…On completion of training…evaluate the effectiveness of programme…compare performance with previous performance…motivational effect…set new goal…plan new training programme.*

SKILLS AND TECHNIQUES

5. (a) A good response will include specific and detailed explanations relevant to open and closed skills.

Examples are often included to highlight understanding in context; this may be generic or linked to a specific skill/technique.

Points highlighted:
Open – dependent on different variables eg weather, ground conditions, opponents externally placed eg a corner kick in football.
Closed – Internally paced, fewer variables, eg a service in badminton.

(b) **Features of a skilled performance**

A good response will include reference to the range of qualities that are evident in a skilled/model performance **of this skill**.

A link to relevant factors may include: executed at the correct time with consistency, fluency, economy of effort. Movements/application of skill seems effortless, model performer uses skill with a degree of confidence, with few unforced errors and makes appropriate decisions about when to use the skill when under pressure etc.

(c) **Motivation/Concentration/Feedback**

In this respect the candidate should give a detailed synopsis of how each factor impacted upon their learning and/or their application of **this skill/technique**. Merit should be given according to depth/quality/relevance of explanations offered.

Motivation – A good response will include details of being internally (intrinsic)/externally (extrinsic) motivated to learn/achieve success. Being motivated enables the performer to be self driven to listen to instruction and act on it, it helps the performer to be self determined/give of their best even if development programme challenging and not to worry if mistakes are made while developing the skill. Motivation would ensure perseverance throughout training session and for the duration of the programme.

Concentration – A good response will include details of the need to concentrate/focus on instruction/demonstration offered to ensure effective execution/application of skill or technique, promotes progression/adaptation of skill or technique, ensures bad habits are not formed/eradicated, enables the performer to apply the skill appropriately in different training contexts.

NOTE: A link to stages of learning, and Model Performers may be made in reference to either of the above factors.

(d) **The importance of monitoring and reviewing**

A good response will highlight the differences/benefits of the purpose of monitoring the ongoing process. Such as – reference to appropriate data methods to facilitate comparison of improvements, achieving targets set, gaining and acting on feedback, aids motivation, ensures further challenge and progress.

Importantly, the response must include reference to reviewing performance ie summative progress. However reference to the evaluation of the whole process ie the impact of the training/development programme/programme of work should be highlighted. Judgement on the success/effectiveness of the programme used plus judgements on the success/ effectiveness to whole performance must be clearly defined.

A good response will highlight the impact of skill technique development to whole performance development.

6. (a) **Methods of practice**

The response offered will be wide ranging and may include the candidate's choice of skill/technique identified for development.

The response must include details of the considerations/critical debate about the selection and appropriateness of the methods of practice/development programme followed. In this respect the candidate should be convincing in their argument about why one method was selected in preference to another ie the 'process' should be obvious and justified.

The methods chosen should be detailed with reference made to their use at the appropriate stage of learning. Some of the following considerations should be included in the justification of use at each stage: skill complexity/classification, Model Performer, feedback, goal setting…etc.

For example… *At the cognitive stage – many shadow/repetition practices were incorporated to ensure…etc. At the associative stage some shadow/repetition practices progressing to combine drills, etc. At the automatic stage of learning more pressure/problem solving drills were used to advance and challenge learning and performance development.*

A link to other relevant factors may include: whole part, whole gradual build up, mass/distributed, closed/open contexts etc.

(b) **Data methods**

The method selected may be wide ranging. A good response will include detail about the process. In a systematic way the candidate should exhibit sound level of critical thinking by highlighting what was done.

NOTE: some data tools used may feature in more than one collection type; this is acceptable. Also diagrams of methods used often feature to support depth of answer.

Acceptable examples of methods of gathering data may include:
Movement Analysis: Video, Obs.C/list, Match Analysis Sheets/scattergram/questionnaires, PAR sheets, Comparison to Model Performers etc.
Mechanical Analysis: Video, Obs.C/list, questionnaires, PAR sheets of force, levers, propulsion etc.
Consideration of Quality: reflecting on movement skill execution being controlled/fluent, or fast/slow etc via video, Obs.C/list, questionnaires, PAR sheets, Comparison to Model Performers.

NOTE: in the candidate's description of the method(s) selected the relevance of criteria must be justified. For example if the candidate names a 'mechanical analysis sheet' but proceeds to highlight the details pertaining to a movement analysis method such as Match Analysis Sheet then this exhibits poor acquired knowledge and understanding.

(c) Development needs may be described with reference to the application of the skill in the WHOLE performance context. This may include quantitative evidence, ie the % success rate of specific skill.

The candidate may describe how their whole performance was affected.
For example… *My inaccurate shooting meant that I often missed the shot…this in turn affected my confidence and execution of other skills…on looking at my scatter gram I had a high % of my shots landing out…a poor preparation phase in my smash meant that I was not behind the shuttle when hitting it – this caused me to lose power…therefore my development needs were to improve my transfer of weight from front to back foot.*

(d) **Principles of effective practices**

The response must show applied knowledge of the Principles of effective practice. Reference should be made to some of the following:
• Setting clear objectives
• Strengths and weaknesses consideration
• Awareness of model performer
• Achievable stages and progression
• Effect of boredom and fatigue
• Intensity of practice
• Work rest ratio

Often the acronym S.M.A.R.T.E.R. features in the candidate's answers.
For example… *Practice should be specific, measurable, attainable, time related, exciting and regular…as my programme was specific it helped me to achieve success…I could target the specific parts of my technique that need most improvement. I know to set targets and raise them once…this ensures my practice was motivating etc.*

STRUCTURES, STRATEGIES AND COMPOSITIONS

7. (a) **Structure, strategy or composition**

The candidate must describe the Structure, Strategy or Composition. Some will also make reference possibly to the role they played within it.

These may include:
- Basketball-fast break…zones…1-3-1…horse shoe offence…man/man defence.
- Football 4-2-4/4-3-3/3-5-2/3-5-1.
- Badminton front-back-side-side.
- Gymnastics particular sequence-routine.
- Volleyball-Rotational setter, Specialist setter, W service reception formation.
- Hockey penalty corner-passing it back to the 'injector' on the post.

For example… *In tennis I used a serve volley strategy… I would serve fast and hard to opponent…follow my serve… get into net and position quickly… use a volley to win point… from opponents return. Hockey…I played in a zone defence where I had to cover a particular area of the pitch.*

(b) The responses will be wide ranging and will depend on the choice of SSTC selected. Responses should provide a description of the problem they faced.

For example… *In basketball we were playing a 2-1-2 zone…opposition had good outside shooters…scoring frequently, in football we played a 4-4-2 formation…we found when attacking all 4 players in midfield would be up the park…supporting the forwards…when the attack broke down the opposition often broke quickly…our midfield were slow to get back…our defence was under pressure…in volleyball we had two people who were unable to provide effective sets for our spikers…this meant when they were in the setting position, we were unable to build an attack and win points.*

(c) **The importance of adapting and refining a structure, strategy or composition in response to performance demands**

The responses will be wide ranging and will depend on the choice of structure, strategy or composition selected. Responses may repeat the description of the problem they faced. They should then show evidence of problem solving and decision making to make their whole performance more effective.

For example… *In basketball we were playing a 2-1-2 zone…opposition had good outside shooters …scored frequently…we changed to half court man/man defence to stop them…this led to less successful shots as they were under more pressure…forced them to try and drive to basket. They made more mistakes…scored less baskets as they were poor at driving to basket…we won more turnovers and could attack more.*

(d) The response will include descriptions of particular methods to gather information on effectiveness followed by an explanation of the validity of the method used – these could include video-games analysis – observation schedules – knowledge of results – criteria checklists – statistics – personal reflection – feedback – internal/external feedback – comparison to previous information gathered – match analysis sheets.

For example… *In basketball… we used a criteria checklist…all aspects of fast break…data was collected from a game this then allowed…comparison to previous…to see if we had improved its effectiveness.*

8. (a) **Structure and Strategy Fundamentals**

The following may be referred to or listed.
Using space in attack and defence, pressure opponents, tempo of play, speed in attack, delay in defence and principles of play (width, depth and mobility), previous knowledge of opposition or conditions strengths and weaknesses of own team or/and opposition.
The importance should be justified and show both acquired and applied knowledge.

For example… *In basketball I wanted to play a fast tempo game…attack quickly…so I made sure that on each opportunity we tried to play a fast break… to catch the defence out… score a quick basket…create an overload situation…before the defence was organised properly.*

Structure and Compositional Fundamentals

The following may be referred to or listed.
Design form, developing motifs, using repetition, variation and contrast, interpreting stimulus in developing performance, using space effectively, using creativity in performance.
The importance should be justified and show both acquired and applied knowledge.

For example… *In dance I started with a simple step motif…took me forwards then back to starting position…then sideways… back to starting…I established this as a simple core motif…then I developed a second core motif…this time a jumping pattern…then I began to mix and play with both core motifs…to add interest to my dance…give my dance variety and quality of movement contrasts.*

(b) **Recognising the demands of individual roles during performance**

For example… *In basketball as a centre my role was to rebound the ball in offence and block out in defence…shoot close to basket…to link with forwards and guards in passing movements in and around key.*

The candidate should give details of the specific responsibilities a particular role demands. This can include attacking, defensive responsibilities or, in a creative environment, decisions a performer might make during a performance to adjust positioning or even timing.
The candidate may also describe a structure, strategy and composition they have performed within, but it is important that their ROLE within this is identified.

The possible structure, strategy or composition might be:
- fast break/zones/1-3-1/horse shoe office in basketball/man-man defence
- Football 4-2-4/4-3-3/3-5-2
- Badminton front-back-side-side
- Gymnastics particular sequence – routine
- Volleyball – rotational setter
- Hockey penalty corner

(c) (i) **The strength identified must relate to the role performed**

For example…*In my role as specialist setter in my volleyball team I was able to convert even bad/poor passes into attacking opportunities for my spikers…I was able to make quick decisions about where the set was going in order to avoid the block or to give my spikers the opportunity to capitalise on spaces or weaknesses on my opponent's side of the net…I was also able to judge what type of set my spikers preferred.*

An explanation of the impact of this strength on performance must be given, for example, *My strength allowed me to give good attacking service to my spikers ensuring every attacking opportunity gave us the chance of winning the point....put my opponents under pressure....added the element of disguise...confusing the blockers.*

(ii) <u>**The weakness identified must relate to the role performed**</u>

For example...*Within my role as specialist setter, I caused many rotational faults by moving at the wrong time or being in the wrong position as the service was taken. This caused problems in my team and lost us points...The impact of this on our performance was that the opposition began to target the moving player – causing more confusion and disagreement within our team.*

(d) <u>**Weaknesses Addressed**</u>

The responses offered will be wide ranging and will depend on the choice of role and the weakness(es) identified. The responses should be a description of the programme of work followed but this must be relevant to weakness mentioned in part (c) (ii)

For example... *We worked as a team with no opponents walking through the timing and positioning of players at service reception with just a feed from the other side of the net. We progressed to develop this when our team was serving...*

Various methods of training/practice may be described – reference should be made either as individuals or as part of a team...a range of development programmes will be evident-the structure should be evident as well as the content. Responses must show critical thinking and relevant decision making and should reduce the effect of weakness(es) on performance.

HIGHER PHYSICAL EDUCATION 2013

In the Higher Physical Education examination candidates will have answered from the perspective of their experiences in a wide variety of activities. To produce an activity specific marking scheme would result in an enormous document which would be extremely cumbersome and time-consuming to use and which could never realistically cover all possibilities.

In relation to **all** questions it should be noted that the relevance of the content in the candidates' responses will depend on:

- the activity selected
- the performance focus
- the training/development programme/programme of work selected
- the practical experiences of their course as the contexts for answers.

PERFORMANCE APPRECIATION

1. (a) <u>**Nature and Demands:**</u>

Nature: Individual/team. The duration of the game/event. The number of player(s) / performers involved. A spectator / audience event. Indoor/outdoor. Directly / indirectly competitive. Objective / subjective scoring system in application. Codes of conduct.

Demands: Technical, Physical, Mental and Special. Candidates may demonstrate acquired Knowledge and Understanding across all related demands or focus on one more comprehensively. Similarly, candidates may demonstrate acquired Knowledge and Understanding in respect of the unique game/event demands or emphasise the demands unique to the role/solo/duo performance relative to the activity selected.

<u>**Special Performance Qualities**</u>

The responses will be wide ranging and relevant to the activity selected. Candidates may demonstrate acquired Knowledge and Understanding in respect of the specific role/solo related demands necessary for an effective performance.

Reference to the application of a series of complex skills will impact on performance in competitive situations. For example, *In relation to role demands,... as a central defender I am pushed to my limits in the later stages of the game... it is essential that I time my tackles or I will give away penalties... I need to control the ball artistically to wrong foot my opponent and get the ball out of danger areas... etc.*

In relation to solo demands...*as a gymnast I know that my tumbling routine has many complex skills that need to be performed in a linked sequence... I need tremendous focus as often I will be pushing myself to the limits... etc... most importantly I need to add flair and fluency in my routine to attract the best marks from the judges... etc.*

Candidates who are elite performers may demonstrate acquired Knowledge and Understanding in respect of the application of strategy/composition at appropriate times to ensure an effective performance. Often this link is made in cognisance of Knowledge of Results and or Knowledge of Performance. For example, *reflecting on previous performances we knew to double mark their key player as this would... etc...*
By applying a man to man strategy immediately would tire them out and give us an advantage... etc... reflecting on my previous results I had to decide which solo piece to execute that would attract the best marks from the judges, etc...

Consideration of activity challenges and qualities demanded

The responses will be wide ranging and relevant to the activity selected. Candidates should demonstrate acquired Knowledge and Understanding in respect of the specific challenges of the activity selected and importantly demonstrate critical thinking by exemplifying the qualities required as a performer to meet the challenges highlighted.

Reference to the type of activity may be evident to set the scene, for example, an individual/team activity, an indoor/outdoor activity, playing competitively or as leisure pursuit will help qualify the candidate's explanations. For example, in relation to activity challenges, ... *in squash the challenges I face are demanding... the aim of the game is to get to lead to 9 points over my opponent... a win = best out of three games... the challenges requires me to play the ball against at least one wall away from my opponent to gain points without obstructing my opponents route to the ball... The qualities I require are skill related - with high levels of agility and reaction time as I... etc I require high levels of mental skills to ensure I make tactical decisions, patience being crucial as I outmanoeuvre my opponent to take point advantage...*

(b) Model performance comparison

A good response will include reference to the range and qualities that are evident in a model performer's repertoire. Reference may be made across the range of demands required in performance ie – technical, physical, skill and mental related.

In relation the demand selected relevant points may come from both 'like / unlike' perspective. For example, *unlike a Model Performer I do not have a repertoire of skills to meet the technical demands of..., I fail to execute my... at the correct time and lack consistency, fluency. Unlike the Model Performer I look clumsy by comparison and lack economy of movement... they make everything look so effortless... their movements / application of skills are used at the right time. However, like the Model Performer I can manage my emotions. I rarely display bad temper and concentrate fully on my game/role... Etc.*

(c) Organising of training

Within the response examples could include:
Knowledge of previously stated strengths and weaknesses. Setting of objectives/preparation for competitive event. Decisions taken as a result of the performance weaknesses/strengths reflective of appropriate training/development method(s) and or selected training regimes. Training considerations offered should reflect and offer examples based on the complexity of identified weaknesses, stage of learning, complexity of stacks etc.
Training considerations may include some or more of the following: training in/out of the activity/conditioning approach, integrated training.

Programme of work must include identification and consideration of performance strengths as well as development needs.
The training programme offered may reflect the development of a technical / skill related or fitness aspect of performance. For example, in badminton the aim could be to develop the drop shot (technical) whilst developing improved footwork (agility)

(d) Mental factors

Candidates may demonstrate acquired Knowledge and Understanding by referencing the ability to manage emotions, deal with cognitive/somatic anxiety. Level of arousal – over or under arousal. Handling stress affected by self confidence, motivation / concentration etc.

Positive and Negative influences of mental factors

A good response will highlight the potential effects that positive and negative mental factors have on performance.

For example, *a positive influence* will impact upon performance by increasing state of mind/state of arousal and so enable the performer to produce sound levels of effectiveness/perform at maximum potential level/handle the pressure and remain calm/make appropriate decisions and enable appropriate actions in response to the immediate situation. There may be heightened awareness/confidence/early preparedness/few unforced errors/sustained performance standards and production of consistent application of skills to deal with the performance context. Reference may also be made to external factors such as crowd, level of competition and rewards.

Conversely – *a negative influence* will impact performance in producing an ineffective/erratic and unconfident performance. Other points raised may include apprehension/suffering cognitive and or somatic anxiety/the feeling of defeat before the event has begun etc.

A link to other relevant factors may include; bad temper, nervousness/lack of commitment/committing fouls, over confidence/lacking confidence etc.

The candidate should highlight the specific aspect of mental fitness, such as dealing with cognitive/somatic anxiety, managing emotions, level of arousal – over or under arousal. The selected factor must be relevant and the effect on performance justified. For example, *cognitive anxiety affected my self confidence, motivation/concentration prior to me starting my game... The very thought of going on court made me panic... I could not overcome my fear and so... etc.* Accompanying the examples offered there should be sufficient depth and quality of explanation to exhibit applied Knowledge and Understanding in context.

2. (a) Special Qualities

In relation to the special performance quality selected, a detailed personal explanantion should be offered. In this respect the candidate may elect to answer from the viewpoint of having a positive or negative effect on performance. Similarly the explanation could be offered via a synopsis of strengths and weaknesses OR strengths only OR a comparative synopsis via a model performer.

Reference may be made to the ability to create opportunity, disguise intent, make performance look more dynamic, apply flair, had the ability to choreograph routines/link complex skills etc. For example, in tennis: *these special qualities helped me to fake my intent and so wrong foot my opponent... I used disguise to wrong foot my opponent who anticipated a smash and I instead played a dropshot.* In trampolining: *my routine was exciting to watch and this helped me gain more points from the judges.*

(b) Physical, Personal and Technical Qualities:

In relation to any of the qualities selected a detailed personal explanation should be included in the candidate's response. In this respect the candidate may elect to answer from the viewpoint of having a positive or negative affect on performance. Similarly, the description could be offered via a summary of strenghts and weaknesses OR strengths only OR a comparative summary via a model performer.

For example, should the candidate select:

Physical: Reference may be made to more than one aspect of fitness. To support KU the candidate must explain how the selected aspect of fitness affected performance. For example, *my high levels of CRE, Speed End helped me*

*maintain pace and track my opponents continuously... etc...
my poor flexibility makes it difficult for me to... Unlike a
model performance my lack of power meant that, etc*

And/or

Personal: Reference may be made to qualities, for example,
height helped me to win rebounds consistently. Other
acceptable personal qualities such as being
decisive/determined/confident/ competitive etc, *put me at
an advantage and intimidated my opponents, etc.*

(c) Integrated training
The response should typically describe a combination from
the following:

Physical (preparation of the body)
Technical (skills and techniques)
Personal (motivation and personal goals)
Special (achieving peak performance)
Mental (rehearsal, imagery, visualisation)
Strategic/compositional planning (structures, strategies and
composition)

For example, *in badminton I wanted to develop the drop shot
while improving my footwork (agility)... I trained in the activity
using repetition drills to improve my drop shot... I also combined
this with specific agility drills to improve my footwork.*

(d) **Importance of analysing and interpreting results for
preparation and monitoring of training programmes**
The responses will include the results arising from the
information gathered and could include reference to specific
demands for the activity or perhaps the role within the
activity. For example, reference could be made to the
importance of analysing and interpretation of results. This
allows the candidate to establish pre training fitness levels
and what they need to work on making specific reference to
their strengths and weaknesses in terms of fitness. It also
provides a bench mark to work on. Specific and realistic
targets can be set over a planned period of time. It also
allows for the planning on a relevant training programme
applying the principles of training. Knowledge of fitness
levels before training allows comparison to be carried out
with post training results. This also allows monitoring to
take place to see if the selected training programme has been
successfully managed and carried out.

PREPARATION OF THE BODY

3. (a) **Principles of training – Specificity and Progressive
Overload**
The answer must refer to both the principles of training.
Most of the following points should be referred to:
Specificity – to the demands of the activity / role within
activity / person / performance / strengths and weaknesses /
types and relevant aspects of fitness / types of training.

Progressive overload – frequency / intensity / duration.
The candidate does not have to answer this part of the
question relative to a specific activity but candidates who do
should be given the appropriate credit.
You will probably have detail or description of how they
were applied to programme and also explanation and
justification why they were considered.

For example, *I made sure the training was specific to the
aspect of fitness / weakness identified... also to the demands of
activity... I planned my programme to be specific to my
anaerobic energy system because... by training the specific
muscle groups required for effective performance I was able
to... I trained 3 times per week with rest every other... allowed
body to recover... applied overload after week 3... increased
number of repetitions by 20 % for 10 to 12 so that I...*

(b) **Physical aspects of fitness**
You would expect the candidate to select an aspect of
physical fitness to show relevant Knowledge and
Understanding to support the answer. The candidate may
choose one aspect of physical fitness from the following list.

Physical fitness – Aerobic-Anaerobic Endurance / Muscular
Endurance / Flexibility / Speed / Strength / Power / Speed
Endurance / Strength Endurance

The candidate must explain the effect the weakness had on
performance to access the full range of marks.
For example, *in football poor levels of Cardio Respiratory
Endurance prevented me from tracking back and helping my
defence... as well as supporting the attackers... throughout the
whole game... Having poor strength as a defender hindered me
when I had to jump and challenge for high balls and crosses...
and winning tackles against the opposition
Low levels of speed restricted my ability to run quickly into
spaces... giving me less time to make correct decisions...and
giving me less time... under more pressure to execute crosses
into the box.*

(c) **Skill related aspects of fitness**
You would expect the candidate to select an aspect of skill
related fitness to show relevant Knowledge and
Understanding to support the answer. The candidate may
choose one aspect of skill related fitness from the following
list.

Skill related fitness: reaction time / agility / co-ordination /
balance / timing / movement anticipation.

The candidate **must explain the effect** the weakness had
on performance to access the full range of marks.
For example, *in badminton having poor agility prevents me
from moving quickly... to reach the shuttle or change direction
if necessary and return the shuttle to put my opponent under
pressure... poor timing prevents me from connecting with the
shuttle in the correct place and allowing me to execute the shot
correctly... decreasing my chances of a successful outcome...
Low levels of balance stop me from transferring my weight
accurately... minimising my ability to execute... a range of
techniques... with maximum power.*

(d) **Appropriate methods of training to improve physical /
skill related and mental fitness**
The candidates responses will be wide ranging and depend
on the choice of activity and the type or aspect of fitness
selected. Various methods of training could be chosen.
Candidates must describe in detail one session. Training
could be within activity/outwith/combination and involve
some of the following methods: fartlek/continuous /
conditioning/interval/circuit/weight training/plyometrics.

For example, *when improving my aerobic endurance for
swimming... warm up of 8 lengths multi stroke... then main
set... I used continuous training as I completed an 800m
swim... I used interval training for swimming 6x50 metre swim
with a minute rest between each set...then sub set... 6x50... 45
sec recovery. This was appropriate because it enables high
intensity work combined with rest to allow me to train for a
longer period of time and thus gaining greater benefits from
training. This is an example where the candidate incorporates
two types of training for one aspect of fitness*

4. (a) **Physical skill related and mental types of fitness**
The candidate should select one aspect within each type of
fitness and show relevant Knowledge and Understanding to
support the answer.
Physical fitness – Cardio Respiratory Endurance – speed –
muscular endurance – flexibility – stamina – strength –
aerobic – anaerobic endurance – speed endurance – power

Skill related fitness – reaction time – agility – co-ordination – balance – timing – movement anticipation
Mental fitness – level of arousal – rehearsal – managing emotion – visualisation – motivation – determination – anxiety/managing stress/concentration
All responses must make reference to how the type or aspect(s) chosen relate to effective performance in the activity.
Physical fitness – for example, *in football a high level of Cardio Respiratory Endurance and speed endurance allowed me to track back and help my defence... out as well as support the attackers... throughout the whole game... also having good strength as a defender allowed me to jump and challenge for high balls and crosses... and win tackles against the opposition.*
Skill related fitness – for example, *in badminton having good quality agility will allow me quick movement... to reach the shuttle or change direction if necessary and return the shuttle to put my opponent under pressure – also... good timing will allow me to connect with the shuttle in the correct place and allow me to execute the shot correctly... hopefully leading to a successful outcome.*
Mental fitness – for example, *in basketball as the ball carrier by managing my emotions I was able to handle the pressure my opponent was putting on me when closely marking... I was able to make the correct decision and carry out the correct pass to my team mate successfully... when I was also taking a free throw by managing my emotions and rehearsing my routine in my mind... I was able to execute the free throws successfully.*

(b) **Appropriate methods of training to improve physical / skill related and mental fitness**
The candidates responses will be wide ranging and depend on the choice of activity and the type or aspect of fitness selected. Various methods of training could be chosen.
Training could be within activity/out with/combination and involve some of the following methods: fartlek/ continuous/ conditioning/interval/circuit/weight training/relaxation/ breathing/rehearsal.
For example, *I used interval training to improve my CRE for swimming... session lasted 90 minutes... warm up of 8 lengths multi stroke... then some stroke development... then main set... 15×100 metre swim with a minute rest between each set... then sub set... 6×50... 45 sec recovery*

When describing their training programme candidates should refer to the duration, frequency and intensity. If the candidate describes one session the maximum marks which could be allocated are two marks

(c) **Adaption to training programme**
Candidates may make reference to the changes they have made however they should not be penalised if no reference is made to the changes. The response must refer to why changes were made to the student's training programme.
Reference could be made to the following:
To provide qualitative or quantitative details of the effectiveness of training programme
To ensure progression and challenge while training and to ensure my fitness does not plateau.
Consider changing intensity of training programme
To ensure motivation stays high while training
To make sure short term goals are achieved
To prevent boredom and provide variety
To return to training after injury or absence from training

For example, *I applied overload after week 3 of my training programme... I did this by increasing the number of sets because I was finding my training too easy and knew I needed to keep forcing my body to adapt and get fitter... this prevented boredom and kept my motivation high.*

(d) **The monitoring process**
A good response will show knowledge about the purpose and importance of the process. It may provide qualitative or quantitative details of whether the training is effective/working – it can substantiate the specific fitness progress – explanations may include – provide evidence to compare progress/targets/improvements – enables changes to be made – ensure future targets – allows for identification of future needs – further challenges – promotes motivation – whether training method was appropriate – deciding if training was at correct intensity – whether short term or long term goals had been achieved.

SKILLS AND TECHNIQUES

5. (a) Description of method used must be offered; a diagram will often feature to support answer. Students should justify the appropriateness of the method describes to enable either qualitative or quantitate details of performance progress.

   In context of the answer, candidates should reference the *'process'* ie **HOW** the data was collected. A narrative account of **what** was done and **why** should be obvious; thus demonstrating logical thinking. *Whole* performance skills/fitness/qualities may be gathered via reliable methods such as video, performance profiles, scatter gram, Match Analysis Schedule, etc.
   A good response must include reference to whole performance (initial data). To substantiate claims reference could be made to one of the following methods:
   Movement Analysis (Observation checklist, Match Analysis sheet)
   Video – comparison of your performance with that of a model performer. The video allowed playback, freeze frame.
   Questionnaire: questions should be relevant to and have responses such as 'done well', 'needs improvement' or mark your performance on a graded scale.
   For example:
   By using video analysis with my general observation schedule I was able to see for myself all areas of my game... this meant I had an accurate picture of my performance which I could rewind and play over again to ensure my data collection was reliable

   This provides evidence to compare progress/targets/improvements... a permanent record, can be used time and time again, aids motivation, and ensures further challenge and progression, information can be gathered at the beginning/middle and end etc.
   If a candidate describes a method of data collection for a specific skill or technique then no marks should be awarded.

   (b) A different method of data analysis must be chosen AND must relate to a specific skill or technique.

   Reference could be made to one of the following methods:
   Preparation/Action/Recovery: Mechanical Analysis of force, levers, propulsion etc
   Consideration of Quality: reflecting on whether your skill or technique was controlled / fluent or fast/slow?
   Scattergram – the outcome of every overhead clear is recorded on court diagram.
   Video – Comparison of your performance with that of a model performer. The video allowed playback, freeze frame.

   Appropriate methods of data collection
   The response should focus on the appropriateness of the method described. Students must justify why the approach was appropriate. Reference should enable either qualitative or quantitative details of performance progress.

For example, *this provides evidence to compare progress/targets/improvements… a permanent record, can be used time and time again, aids motivation, and ensures further challenge and progress, information can be gathered at the beginning/middle and end etc. When using a video there is the opportunity to benefit from using the slow motion, pause facility to enable accurate observations.*

(c) **Principles of effective practice**

The candidate's response should demonstrate sound KU about Principles of Effective Practice with exemplification of how and **why** these were applied. In this context both acquired and applied Knowledge is examined.

The candidate will make reference to the following principles such as…practice needs to show progression to ensure targets were reached/enabled refinement/remediation/ or minimized regression and were focussed on specific strengths and weaknesses, this would increase motivation, improve confidence.
Consideration of work rest ratio to ensure fatigue did not negatively influence performance development may also be included. As may for progression within practices and the need for variety with programme of work.

Some students may also refer to acronym SMARTER. Practices should be specific, measurable etc. Again they should be used to discuss why these were applied as part of the performance development process.

(d) The answer should focus on the performance development process. However, some candidates might make reference to performance developing within the whole performance context.

Motivation/Concentration/Feedback

The candidate should give a detailed synopsis of how **each** factor impacted upon their *learning* and their *application* of skill/technique. Merit should be given according to depth/quality/relevance of explanations offered.
NOTE – *It is likely that similar points may be referenced/exemplified in relation to discrete factor.*

Motivation: A good response will include details of being internally (intrinsic)/externally (extrinsic) motivated to learn/achieve success. Being motivated enables the performer to be self driven to listen to instruction and act on it, it helps the performer to be self determined/give of their best/come from behind/respond to immediate problems/competitive challenges/not worry if mistakes are made and re channel focus
Concentration: A good response will include details of the need to concentrate/focus on instruction/demonstration offered to ensure effective execution/application of skill or technique, promotes progression/adaptation of skill or technique, ensures bad habits are not formed/eradicated, enables the performer to perform their role and apply their skills appropriately, promotes the ability to read play/make effective decisions/adapt to the immediate situation etc.
In the context of games, concentration enables the performer to stick to role related duties/application of structure/strategy/game plan etc.
Feedback: A good response will include details of receiving internal (kinaesthetic), feedback to progress/refine skill or technique OR receiving/giving external feedback (visual/verbal/written), to progress/refine skill or technique of self or that of others.
Feedback should be positive/immediate to promote confidence/success in manageable amounts and be focused on the area being developed.

6. *(a)* **Analysis of strengths in whole performance**

The quality of the analysis offered by the candidate should focus on the strengths within the whole performance context. There might be comparisons to that of a Model Performer or may reflect a statistical percentage of success rate when performing.
Irrespective of the approach taken, the candidate must demonstrate critical thinking by offering a degree of authenticity in their analysis.
Candidates may emphasise how their whole performance was affected. For example, *my accurate shooting meant that I… this in turn affected my confidence and execution of other skills… looking at my scattergram I had a high % of my shots landing…*
In badminton, my high serve was a strength in my performance as I could always land it in the back tram lines of the court…

(b) **Identification of weaknesses within a skill/technique**

The candidate should describe in some detail the specific weakness(es) identified within a skill or technique. They may compare their execution of the skill/technique to that of a Model Performer or may reflect a statistical percentage of success rate when performing.

Candidate should refer specifically to the effects of weakness(es) while executing the skill or the impact of this weak skill on the whole performance or indeed BOTH.

For example:
… looking at my smash which was a weakness… a poor preparation phase… meant that I was not behind the shuttle when hitting it… this caused me to lose power… and my opponent found it easy to return the shuttle. A link to other factors such as reduced confidence, affected other parts of game/performance may be evident.

(c) **Course of action**

The response should focus on the justification of the candidate's choice of methods of practice.

The response must indicate details of the considerations/critical debate about the selection and appropriateness of the methods of practice/development programme followed. In this respect the candidates should be convincing in their argument about **why** one method was selected in preference to another ie the 'process' should be obvious and justified.
The course of action followed should be detailed with reference to **some** of the following considerations:
Stages of Learning
Skill complexity
Skill classification (open/closed)
Model Performer
Feedback
Goal setting
Methods of practice

Methods of practice references may include actual description of the work carried out over a period of time. For example, *as I was at the cognitive stage – I used many shadow/repetition practices to ensure – etc. At the associative stage I used some shadow/repetition practices progressing to combination drills… etc. At the automatic stage of learning I knew to use more pressure/problem solving drills as these would challenge me more… etc. I found the skill very difficult so decided to use gradual build up as this would… etc. In weeks 1 and 2, I concentrated more on simple drills… in weeks 3 and 4, I progressed to more complex drills such as… etc this built my confidence as I reached my target of… etc.*

(d) Relevant description of simple and complex type of skill. The description should include details appropriate to the skills selected.

Simple – requiring few sub routines, no element of danger = forward roll in gymnastics.
Complex – many sub routines, with a number of different variables, element of danger = front somersault in gymnastics.

Candidates may make reference to other types of skill classification such as:

Open skills – generally more complex, dependant on different variables, externally paced eg a corner kick in football.
Closed skills – generally less complex, internally paced, no clear beginning or ending, eg a drive in golf.
Discrete – clear beginning and end, requiring fine motor skills.
Serial – a complex, combination of discrete skills which are performed in sequence, produces a unique skill such as lay up in Basketball.
Continuous – generally more complex, no clear pattern of beginning or end such as swimming.

However, candidates must always make the link back to simple and complex skills.

STRUCTURES, STRATEGIES AND COMPOSITION

7. (a) **Select a relevant structure, strategy or composition**
The candidate must describe the Structure, Strategy or Composition. Some will also make reference possibly to the role they played as well.
These will include fast break/zones/1-3-1/ horseshoe offence in basketball/man/man defence
Football – 4-2-4/4-3-3/3-5-2
Badminton – front-back-side-side
Gymnastics particular sequence – routine
Tennis – serve-volley
Volleyball – rotation
Hockey – penalty corner
For example, *in tennis I used a serve volley strategy – I would serve fast and hard to opponent – follow my serve – get into net and position quickly – use a volley to win point – from opponents return.*

(b) **Weaknesses effect on performance:**

The answers must include the problem faced when applying this SSC. Some candidates may answer by referring to the weakness(es) as a team or as an individual. They must show critical thinking by offering a degree of authenticity in their analysis and should make reference as to how their whole performance was affected.
For example:
My backhand volley was poor - made most errors from this technique - usually went into net or out of court - lost many points - poor second serve - often too short - opponents exploit this leading to lost points - exploitation by opponent - passed on many occasions. Also a link to other factors such as reduced confidence, lack of fitness etc may be evident in the answers.

(c) **Decisions taken to develop performance**
The response should focus on how the student justifies the course of action taken to develop their performance with regards to the problems identified in part (b).
Response should show evidence of problem solving and decision making to make their performance more effective.
For example, the candidates should give details of the

programme of work used to develop performance within this S,S or C. For example, in netball... *the centre pass strategy was not effective because of ineffective dodging from the Wing Attack...we did some work on feinting without defenders...we gradually added passing...then passive defenders...then active defenders. This helped because our confidence increased as the WA became more effective in getting free to receive the first pass.*

(d) Responses must be linked to previous identified weakness(es). Observations should now illustrate the improvements which can be seen in the WHOLE performance.
For example:
I can now see that the centre pass does not break down as the ball is passed to the wing attack near the side line because she is delaying her movement out to the side line, tricking her opponent into thinking she is going to receive the ball near the centre circle. Having practiced this without defenders helped... This means that a secure, safe pass is received and the goal attack is able to time her dodge to receive the next pass near the top of the shooting circle. As a result the strategy of using the WA to create a space to allow a penetrating pass through the middle of the court has been successful.
In our training we understood the importance of creating space so that in the game we were able to...
This allowed our confidence to increase and we began playing with much more determination and our opponents found it difficult to mark us and anticipate what we were going to do next.
Future Needs identified could include reference to adapting or changing the chosen SS or C in response

8. (a) **Structure and strategy fundamentals**
Using space in attack and defence, pressuring opponents, tempo of play, speed in attack, delay in defence and principles of play (width, depth and mobility).
The importance should be justified and show both acquired and applied knowledge.
For example, *in basketball I wanted to play a fast tempo game... attack quickly... so I made sure that on each opportunity we tried to play a fast break... to catch the defence out... score a quick basket... create an overload situation... being perceptive enough to be aware of the placement of defence to try to score before the defence was organised properly.*
Structure and compositional fundamentals
Design for, developing motifs, using repetition, variation and contrast, interpreting stimulus in developing performance, using space effectively, using creativity in performance.
For example, *in dance I started with a simple step motif... took me forwards then back to starting position... then sideways... back to starting... I established this as a simple core motif... then I developed a second motif... this time a jumping pattern... then I began to mix and play with both core motifs... to add interest to my dance... gave my dance variety and quality and some movement contrasts.*
Speed in attack - for example the candidate may (in fast break in basketball) show importance of getting ahead of the ball and the opposition to score an easy lay up / unopposed shot or create overload.
Width depth mobility - in any activity game area a team should successfully cover the width as well as length (depth) of area - also team should adapt and respond to change of either team SSTC or tactics of opposition. Importance of creativity - in gymnastics the types of actions/movements in a particular sequence/linking movements together allow sequence to flow - score more marks.

Using repetition, variation and contrast in dance, similar to above in gymnastics, but using different levels varying the tempo of movements to create an interesting sequence.
In all, the key is to explain the importance when applying to the two features to the selected SSTC.

(b) **Recognising the demands of individual roles during performance**
For example:
In basketball as a centre my role was to rebound the ball in offence... shoot close to the basket... to link with forwards and guards in passing movements in and around key.
The candidate should give details of the specific responsibilities a particular role demands. This can include, attacking, defensive responsibilities or, in a creative environment, decisions a performer might make during a performance to adjust positioning or even timing. The candidate may also describe a structure, strategy or composition they have performed within, but it is important that their ROLE within this is identified.

The possible structure, strategy or composition might be:
fast break/zones/1-3-1/horse shoe offence in basketball/man-man defence
Football 4-2-4/4-3-3/3-5-2
Badminton front – back-side-side
Gymnastic particular sequence – routine
Volleyball – rotation
Hockey penalty corner.

(c) **Recognising the need to maximise strengths within a structure, strategy or composition**
The strengths identified must relate to the role identified.
For example:
In my role as a specialist setter in my volleyball team I had to be able to convert even poor passes into attacking opportunities for my spikers... My volleying is good and consistent and so this is an ideal position for me to play. I had to be able to make quick decisions about where the set was going in order to avoid the block or to give my spikers the opportunity to capitalise on spaces or weaknesses on my opponents' side of the net... I have quick reaction and know my team's preferences and so am able to quickly... I also had to be able to judge what type of set my spikers preferred.

(d) **Structure, strategy or composition**
The response must focus on the description of a different SSCs. The candidate must describe the alternative Structure, Strategy or Composition. Some will also make reference possibly to the role they played as well.

The alternative SSC described should result in the same outcome e.g. 2-1-2 zone as an alternative to half court man to man. Both are defensive.

The student must show evidence of the advantage of using this SSC.
For example...*In comparison to the rotational setter system where everyone has to take responsibility for setting, the alternative specialist setter system has a setter who is skilled enough to give me the type of set I prefer to be able to perform an effective spike...she can play a good set from even a poor first pass...giving my team the chance of more attacking plays.*

HIGHER PHYSICAL EDUCATION 2014

In the Higher Physical Education examination candidates will have answered from the perspective of their experiences in a wide variety of activities. To produce an activity specific marking scheme would result in an enormous document which would be extremely cumbersome and time-consuming to use and which could never realistically cover all possibilities.

In relation to **all** questions it should be noted that the relevance of the content in the candidates' responses will depend on:

- the activity selected
- the performance focus
- the training/development programme/programme of work selected
- the practical experiences of their course as the contexts for answers.

AREA 1: PERFORMANCE APPRECIATION

1. (a) The response should focus on the personal and special demands of performance in the selected activity.

    Reference could be made to some of the following demands:
    - Decision making
    - Strengths and weaknesses
    - Audience/spectators
    - Pressure
    - Type of events
    - Flair
    - Creativity
    - Improvisation
    - Charisma

    For example, *in badminton I am faced with decision making all the time...I have to think about the type of shot to play...in relation to my opponent...the timing of the shot...the technique to use.*

    (b) The response should focus on the technical or physical demands of performance in the selected activity.

    Reference could be made to some of the following demands:
    - Fitness requirements, aspects or types of fitness
    - Types of skills/techniques required for activity
    - Attacking/defending skills
    - Footwork
    - Roles

    For example, *to perform well in badminton I need to have a wide repertoire of skills...in order to perform with a high degree of accuracy...good clears were vital to put my opponent to back of court... it was important to have good footwork in order to reach the return from my opponent.*

    In netball I need agility to be able to dodge quickly away from my opponent to receive a pass from my team mate and also in defence to be able to react to my opponent's attempts to get free to receive a pass.

    (c) **Model Performance**
    The response may focus on the candidate's strengths and weaknesses in comparison to model performance.

    Reference could be made to a range of qualities:
    - Technical
    - Physical
    - Personal
    - Special

For example, *unlike a model performer I do not have a repertoire of skills to meet the technical demands...I fail to execute my ... at the correct time and lack consistency, fluency. Unlike the model performer I look clumsy and lack economy of movement...they make everything look effortless...their movements/application of skills are used at the right time. However, like the model performer, I can manage my emotions...I rarely display bad temper and concentrate fully on my game/role.*

(d) **Course of action**

A good response will include adequate details relevant to the selection and appropriateness of the MOST relevant methods of practice/development/training available. Considerations of different methods will be evident in the process. Examples relevant to selected methods and how this will bring about improvement more commensurate to model performer must be evident.

For example, *to make sure my lay-up shot was more like a model performer. At first I used many repetition drills in a closed environment to ensure I had no pressure...etc. I then progressed to more open practice and used combination/ conditioned drills to ensure refinement of shot, ie against opposition I was more efficient, accurate.*

A link to other relevant factors may include; whole part whole, gradual build up, problem solving contexts, technique classes, body conditioning etc. A good response may typically include other relevant factors to demonstrate knowledge and understanding such as, progression, feedback, target setting, work to rest considerations, stages of learning, complexity of technique being developed, factors affecting performance, principles of effective practice.

Marks should be allocated by a 3/3 split.

2. (a) The response should focus on the importance of managing emotions.

For example, *before my dance competition begins I need to... stay calm...forget about the audience...concentrate on what I aim to do...if I make a mistake during the routine...I must remain focussed...not get upset...affect the rest of the routine ...making sure I walk off stage appropriately and remain composed.*

(b) The response should focus on the performance qualities selected.

In rugby the timing of the jumper is crucial...at a line out...jump to catch the ball at its highest point...to keep possession...start an attack...jump too early and you will make a mistake...opposition could steal ball.

In hockey the speed of the pass at a penalty corner is important...the ball wants to be hit quickly...to reach...the person stopping...allow the player to pass...score a goal...if too slow the opposition will close down quickly.

Marks should be allocated by 2/2 split.

(c) The candidate's response should include full detail about how reliable information was gathered. Analytical thinking should be evident in the selection of the method to match the quality selected.

Gathering data: Description of the method(s) used should be offered; a diagram will often feature to support answer. In context of the answer candidates should reference the 'process' ie how the data was collected. A narrative account of what was done and why should be obvious; thus demonstrating logical thinking.

NOTE 'face validity' of candidates' choice should be accepted in this instance. For example, whole performance

skills/fitness/ qualities may be gathered via reliable methods such as video, performance profiles, scattergrams, match analysis sheet, etc. Most likely, the process offered in the responses will examine Initial data collection then Focussed to value the identification of S&W.

Crucially the link to other relevant factors may include: this information was then used to gain feedback, establish training/practice priorities.

(d) The response should focus on the considerations when setting goals.

For example, *I took into account the length of my training programme ... my level of ability ... my strengths and weaknesses ... my fitness level ... or unrealistic ... not hard enough for me.* Reference could be made to SMARTER.

AREA 2: PREPARATION OF THE BODY

3. (a) Split answer – 2 marks allocated for **each** aspect of mental fitness.

Mental fitness
Full marks should be allocated where the candidate has clearly explained the importance of the aspects of mental fitness.

For example; level of arousal – rehearsal – managing emotion – visualisation – motivation – determination – anxiety/managing stress/ concentration

For example in basketball *as the ball carrier...by managing my emotions I was able to handle the pressure my opponent was putting on me when closely marking...I was able to make the correct decision and carry out the correct pass to my team mate successfully...when I was also taking a free throw by managing my emotions and rehearsing my routine in my mind...I was able to execute the free throw successfully.*

(b) This question is a 2/2 split. 2 marks allocated for each aspect of skill–related fitness.

Skill related fitness
The candidate could choose from: Movement Anticipation, Balance, Reaction Time, Coordination, Agility and Timing. Full marks should be allocated where the candidate has clearly explained the importance of both aspects of skill related fitness. For example; Skill related fitness – for example in badminton having good agility will allow me quick movement ... to reach the shuttle or change direction if necessary and return the shuttle to put my opponent under pressure-also...good timing will allow me to connect with the shuttle in the correct place and allow me to execute the shot correctly...hopefully leading to a successful outcome.

(c) **Principles of training**
The response should show acquired knowledge of the principles of training considered when planning a fitness training programme. Reference should be made to the following:
• Specificity – activity, personal and aspect of fitness
• Overload – frequency, intensity and duration
• Progression
• Rest and recovery
• Reversibility
• Adaptation
• Tedium
• Variation
• Tapering

For example I made sure the training was specific to the weakness identified...also to the demands of the activity because...I trained 3 times per week with rest every other day...this allows my body to recover.

(d) The candidates response should display both acquired and applied KU when discussing the appropriateness of the selected method of training.

The mark allocation will be a 2/4 split.
1 mark awarded for describing a session.
2 marks awarded for description.
4 marks awarded for discussion.

Appropriate methods of training to improve physical/skill related and mental fitness

The candidates response will be wide ranging and depend on the choice of activity and the type or aspect of fitness selected. Various methods of training could be chosen and some candidates may choose one session or a block of time to describe what they did. Training could be within activity/out with/combination and involve some of the following methods: fartlek/continuous/conditioning/interval/circuit/weight training/relaxation/ breathing/rehearsal.

A good response should have good description of the form of training.

Within the activity (conditioning): For example, *in athletics for 800 metre running I did fartlek type training on the track…did 8 laps…jogged the straights and ran the bends … done without stopping … then did 6 short 60 metre sprints with a short 20 metre jog leading into each sprint made demand similar to end of actual race.*

Out with activity could include circuit training/weight training with description of what they did/sets/reps/types of exercise. For example, *to improve my Cardio Respiratory Endurance for my role as a midfielder in hockey…I trained out with activity…carried out some circuit training…doing high intensity work…work rest ratio 1:3…doing a series of exercises…step ups…burpees…continuous running…3 sets of exercises…working on each for 45 seconds.*

Combination of both: continuous training in pool/weight training out of pool with appropriate description of each/involve some of the following methods fartlek/continuous/ conditioning/interval/circuit/weight training/relaxation/breathing/rehearsal. For example, *in swimming I trained using a combination of training within activity and out with activity…within I used interval training…working on developing both anaerobic and aerobic fitness…did warm up…then stroke improvement…main set 6×50 metre swim one minute recovery…sub set 6×50…45 secs recovery…then warm down…out with pool did a weight training circuit…doing a series of exercises…3 sets of exercises…also some work on stepping machines…rowing machines…to improve Cardio Respiratory Endurance.*

Discussion of the appropriateness of selected method

Within activity: can involve specific movements and can develop skills as well as fitness – involve demands of the activity – can also simulate the pressure demands of a competitive situation – can also be fun and motivational.
Out-with activity: can develop both general and specific muscle/fitness– easy to do – minimum of equipment needed.
Combination: some of the above reasons but firmly explained why – variety in different methods – motivational – enjoyable.

4. (a) The candidate must demonstrate both acquired and applied KU in relation to each phase of training.

Phases of training: You would expect the answers to offer some description of what they did in each phase and to explain what each particular stage means, giving specific examples of training covered and **why each phase is different**.

For example in the **preparation phase (preseason)** candidates will refer to general fitness work being developed to build up endurance whereas in the **competition phase (during the season)** they should explain why they are required to work on specific aspects of fitness/skills for competition. Fine tuning of skills and working on specific strategies would be apparent in this phase compared to the preseason where more general of working on skills would happen. In the **transition phase (off season)** you would expect responses to refer to the body recovering after competition and maintaining a general/reasonable level of fitness maybe by doing some alternative activities like swimming or cycling.

Examples in:
Preparation (preseason) could include general running/circuit training/particular drills
Competition (during the season) could include a strength/fitness training program to improve a particular part of fitness which is vital in game or working on a particular penalty corner drill for hockey.
Transition (off season) could include swimming, cycling as an alternative activity and a basic circuit to keep your fitness ticking over.
Reasons for particular differences given between each stage should show relevant KU. For example the **preparation phase (preseason)** is about building up fitness in a general way whereas the **competition phase (during the season)** is about reaching a particular level and then looking at improving specific fitness.

(b) The candidate's response should include detail from method(s) used within and out with the activity.
The mark allocation will be a 3/3 split for within and out with the activity.

Gathering data – The description of methods must be within the activity. A diagram may feature in the answer, for example, a time related observation schedule within football, showing information relevant to the particular aspect selected which was speed endurance/Cardio Respiratory Endurance. In the answer the candidate should make reference to the process as to how the information was gathered. A narrative account of what was done and why should be obvious showing logical thinking. Methods could include video/performance profiles/checklists/scattergrams/Preparation, Action, Recovery/ stroke counts/breath counts/pulse counts/feedback – reliability and validity of method should be apparent.

Methods must come from out with activity. For example, Standardised tests will also be described, these could include:
Physical – 12 minute Cooper test, Sit and reach test, Harvard step test, Bleep test
Skill related – Illinois agility test, ruler drop, alternative hand throw
Mental – questionnaires or self evaluation tests, internal/external feedback.

(c) Candidates are expected to select one training session from their programme and give a description.

The session described may be very specific to one aspect of fitness or be more general in nature.

The candidates responses will be wide ranging and depend on the choice of activity and the type or aspect of fitness selected.

For example, *I used interval training for swimming...warm up of 8 lengths multi stroke...then some stroke improvement...then main set...6 × 50 metre swim with a minute rest between each set...then sub set...6 × 50...45 sec recovery. This was high intensity work combined with rest which allowed me to train for a longer period of time. This was a session to improve speed endurance.*

(d) **The importance of monitoring and reviewing:**
A good response will show knowledge about the purpose and importance of the process. It may provide qualitative or quantitative details of whether the training is effective/working – it can substantiate the specific fitness progress – explanations may include/provide evidence to compare progress/targets/improvements –

...enables changes to be made – ensure future targets/further challenges – promotes motivation – whether training method was appropriate – deciding if training was at correct intensity – whether short term or long term goals had been achieved.

AREA 3: SKILLS AND TECHNIQUES

5. (a) The candidate must include the following points to demonstrate acquired KU of Stages of Learning.

Stages of learning
A good response will include specific reference and appropriate detail with detailed explanations relevant to the stage of learning described. Examples are often included to highlight their understanding in context; this may be generic or linked to a specific skill/technique.

For example, at the cognitive stage a performer will be reliant on a lot of instruction/ feedback. The performer is learning about the sub routines of the skill/technique. Success rate/effectiveness is not refined etc.

At the associative stage, a performer will still be reliant on instruction/feedback but will be developing ability to self evaluate. The performer is more able to link the sub routines of the skill/technique; the execution of the skill is recognisable but the success rate/effectiveness is still not consistent or highly effective, etc.

At the automatic stage, a performer will be less reliant on instruction/feedback with an ability to self evaluate and identify weaknesses. The performer is able to link the sub routines of the skill/technique; the execution of the skill is recognisable with control and consistency etc.

A link to other relevant factors may include: progressions possible from one stage to the next, model/skilled performer etc.

Marks should be allocated by a 2/2 split.

(b) The response must include details of the considerations/critical debate about the selection and appropriateness of the methods of practice/development programme followed. In this respect the candidate should be convincing in their argument about why one method was selected in preference to another ie the 'process' should be obvious and justified.

For example, at the cognitive stage – many shadow/repetition practices were incorporated to ensure ... etc. At the associative stage some shadow/repetition practices progressing to combination drills, etc. At the automatic stage of learning more pressure/problem solving drills were used to advance and challenge learning and performance development.

A link to other relevant factors may include; whole part, gradual build up, mass/distributed, closed/open contexts, etc.

(c) The candidate can select either
• Strengths
• Weaknesses
• Strengths and weaknesses
to access full marks

Strengths and weaknesses
The response must refer to the candidate's strengths and weaknesses when applying their selected skill or technique. References could be made to the following:

Preparation, action, recovery of skill
Execution of skill
Consistency in application of skill
Qualities – technical, physical and practical
Effectiveness of skill
Mechanical principles – balance, centre of gravity, levers
Fluency, control
Timing

For example, *when performing the lay up in basketball, one of my weaknesses was the footwork...when executing the skill I often took off the wrong foot...this led to me being imbalanced...*

(d) **Course of action**
The response should focus on the justification of the candidate's chosen course of action.

The response must indicate details of the considerations/critical debate about the selection and appropriateness of the materials of practice/development programme followed. In this respect the candidates should be convincing in their argument about why one method was selected in preference to another ie the 'process' should be obvious and justified.

The course of action followed should be detailed with reference to some of the following considerations:
• Stages of Learning Skill complexity
• Skill classification (open/closed)
• Model
• Performers
• Feedback
• Goal setting
• Methods of practice

Programme references may include actual description of the work carried out over a period of time.

For example: *As I was at the cognitive stage – I used many shadow/repetition practices to ensure – etc. At the associative stage I used some shadow/repetition practices progressing to combination drills...etc. At the automatic stage of learning I knew to use more pressure/problem solving drills as these would challenge me more...etc. I found the ? skill very difficult so decided to use gradual build up as this would...etc. In weeks 1 & 2, I concentrated more on simple drills...in weeks 3 & 4, I progressed to more complex drills such as...etc this built my confidence as I reached my target of...*

6. (a) **Features of a model performance**
The response must explain the advantages of considering a model performance.

Reference may be made to the following:
Range of qualities – technical, physical, special and personal
Example of high quality performance – few unforced errors, good decision making under pressure
Comparison to own performance – strengths and weaknesses
Motivation
Confidence
Goal setting
Visual picture

For example *I used the Model to help me first of all get a picture in my mind's eye of what I was aiming to do...this helped me set targets and stay motivated to work through my training programme*

(b) 3 marks for description
3 marks for explanation

The response must give detailed description of the method of practice used with relevant explanation as to its appropriateness.

The response must include a description of an appropriate method of practice. These could include:
- Shadow practice
- Opposed/unopposed practice
- Gradual build up
- Whole part whole
- Drills
- Repetition
- Conditioned games
- Small sided games

For example *in badminton I used conditioned games...I played against an opponent where I could win an extra point if I won the rally by using the smash.*

The second response must indicate details of the considerations/critical debate about the selection and appropriateness of the methods of practice/development programme followed. In the respect the candidate should be convincing in their argument about why one method was selected in preference to another ie the 'process' should be obvious and justified.

Reference could be made to some of the following considerations:
- Stages of learning
- Skill complexity/skill classification
- Current Ability level
- Difficulty of practice

For example: *The stages of learning...As I was at the cognitive stage – I used many shadow/repetition practices to ensure that I was able to slow the movement down as I was wanting to get the foundations of the skill correct...At the associative stage I used some shadow/repetition practices progressing to combination drills...this made my work a bit more demanding and game like...At the automatic stage of learning I knew to use more pressure/problem solving drills as these would challenge me more...etc.*

(c) **Whole performance development**
A good response will highlight the impact of skill/technique development to WHOLE performance development. For example a more consistent application/fewer errors/ more points won, a positive benefit including greater confidence etc.

(d) **Motivation/Concentration/Feedback**
In this respect the candidate may give a detailed synopsis of how each factor selected impacted upon their learning and or their application of skill/technique. Merit should be given according to depth/quality/relevance of explanations offered.

Motivation = A good response will include details of being internally (intrinsic)/ externally (extrinsic) motivated to learn/achieve success. Being motivated enables the performer to be self driven to listen to instruction and act on it, it helps the performer to be self determined/give off their best/come from behind/respond to immediate problems/competitive challenges/not worry if mistakes are made and re channel focus.

Concentration = A good response will include details of the need to concentrate/ focus on instruction/demonstration offered to ensure effective execution/application of skill or technique, promotes progression/adaptation of skill or technique, ensures bad habits are not formed/eradicated, enables the performer to perform their role and apply their skills appropriately, promotes the ability to read play/make effective decisions/adapt to the immediate situation... etc. In the context of games, concentration enables the performer to stick to role related duties/application of structure/strategy/game plan...etc.

Feedback = A good response will include details of receiving internal (kinaesthetic) feedback to progress/refine skill or technique OR receiving/giving external feedback (visual/verbal/written/vestibular), to progress/refine skill or technique of self or that of others. Feedback should be positive/immediate to promote confidence/success.

3 marks for each factor discussed.

AREA 4: STRUCTURES, STRATEGIES AND COMPOSITION

7. (a) The candidate must demonstrate acquired KU in their description of a SSTC they have used.

   Structures, strategies and composition
   The candidate must describe in detail the Structure, Strategy or Composition. Some will also make reference possibly to the role they played as well. These will include fast break/zones/1-3-1/horse shoe offence in basketball/man/man defence
   Football – 4-2-4/4-3-3/3-5-2
   Badminton – front-back-side-side
   Gymnastics – particular sequence-routine
   Volleyball – rotation
   Hockey – penalty corner
   Dance – a particular dance or routine used.

   (b) The candidate may answer either as an individual role or as part of a team/group performance.

   Recognising the need to maximise strengths within a structure, strategy or composition. The response should focus on how the candidate made best use of their strengths when applying their SSC.

   The following factors may be apparent in answers – to use particular players with particular roles – strengths of these players – type of opposition – attack/defence being applied by my team or opposition – time restrictions in game – after a particular time or situation in activity – ground/weather conditions – prior or previous knowledge of opponent/s – previous results.

   For example: *When playing basketball we used the three tallest players we had to form the rebound triangle in our zone defence so we could collect rebounds defensively when our opposition missed their shots at the basket.*

   (c) The candidate must be able to describe the weakness(es) they had when applying SSTC and demonstrate detailed discussion on the effect on their performance

   Weaknesses effect on performance: The answers must include their weakness(es). Some candidates may answer by referring to the weakness(es) as a team or as an individual. They must show critical thinking by offering a degree of authenticity in their analysis and should make reference as to how their whole performance was affected.

   For example: *My backhand volley was poor – made most errors from this technique – usually went into net or out of court – lost many points – poor second serve – often too short – opponents exploit this leading to lost points – exploitation by opponent – passed on many occasions.*

Also a link to other factors such as reduced confidence, lack of fitness, etc may be evident in the answers.

Marks should be allocated: 2 for description; 4 for discussion

(d) The candidate must demonstrate relevant critical thinking and decision making to explain how the effect of the weakness(es) were reduced.

Weaknesses addressed: The responses offered will be wide ranging and will depend on the choice of SSTC selected and the weakness(es) identified. The responses could be a description of the programme of work followed but this must be relevant to weakness mentioned.

For example: *for my backhand volley I carried out a skill development programme…partner threw me a ball…play a backhand volley…gradually increased speed and distance… added more pressure…eventually to full speed…then aim for targets on court…two feeders drive me the ball from back of court…alternate backhand/forehand volley…serve to partner and get them to return to backhand side to play volley.*

Various methods of training/practice may be described – reference may be made to possible changes to SSTC either as individuals or as part of a team…a range of development programmes will be evident – the structure should be evident as well as the content – the SSTC may be changed or adapted to overcome weakness(es)…substitute player. Responses must show critical thinking and relevant decision making and should reduce the effect of weakness(es) on performance.

8. (a) Candidates should give a description of the benefits of structure, strategy or composition.

(b) An attempt must be made to do more than describe the limitations of the second structure, strategy or composition. Rather an explanation of the impact on the whole performance as a result of the limitations must be provided

(c) Candidates should show acquired KU as to why it is important to gather information on selected SSTC. They should include some or more of the following.

Information gathering
Find out the strengths and weaknesses of your team/your role in team/of opposition – find out if your SST is effective or requires change – to suit particular needs – to inform decisions about the future – able to plan a programme of practice to implement SST more effectively.

Examples should be given of the strengths and weaknesses identified.

Marks should be awarded 4/2 with emphasis on gathering information.

(d) **Decisions taken to develop performance**
The response should focus on how the candidate justified the course of action taken to develop their performance.

Response should show evidence of problem solving and decision making to make their performance more effective. For example.
The candidate may decide to alter / adapt within the structure, strategy or composition. For example *in football we played a 4-4-2 formation…we found when attacking all 4 players in midfield would be up the park…supporting the forwards…when the attack broke down the opposition often broke quickly…our midfield were slow to get back…our defence was under pressure…we adapted the structure, strategy or composition by having one player…holding in midfield in front*

of back four…one midfield supporting strikers…and two in middle to move back and forward as necessary…this led to a more balanced attack and defence and allowed us to prevent the opposition breaking quickly. Holding midfield was able to delay attack…allows others to get back.

The candidates may decide to follow a programme of work to develop their performance. For example *in netball…the centre pass strategy was not effective because of ineffective dodging from the Wing Attack…we did some work on feinting without defenders…we gradually added passing…then passive defenders…then active defenders.*